Passionate Journey
My Unexpected Life

MARIAN LEONARD TOMPSON
WITH MELISSA CLARK VICKERS

Passionate Journey--My Unexpected Life

By Marian Leonard Tompson

with Melissa Clark Vickers

Hale Publishing, L.P.

1712 N. Forest St.

Amarillo, TX 79106-7017

806-376-9900

800-378-1317

www.iBreastfeeding.com

www.halepublishing.com

Library of Congress Control Number: 2011929109

ISBN-13: 978-0-9833075-7-0

Printing and Binding: Malloy, Inc.

Dedication

To my husband Tom,

Who knew there was a book in me long before I did.

Love you.

Table of Contents

Introduction

April 20, 2009. That's the day I won the lottery. Okay, not really, but it felt like it. That was the day I had an intriguing email from Marian Tompson, one of the seven founders of La Leche League International, which asked simply, "Can we talk?"

I'd been an LLL Leader for 19 years, and for most of those years, I knew the founders only by name and reputation. I'd even seen them at a few International Conferences over the years, and probably shaken hands with all of them at one time or another–no doubt feeling like I was shaking the hands of royalty or celebrities. In more recent years, I've had a few opportunities to work directly with Marian and had gotten to know her a little. I was hearing enough fascinating stories that I started telling her every chance I had that she needed to write a book about her life, and if she needed help to just let me know….

She told me how her husband, Tom, had urged her to do the same, but she had just never gotten around to it–and knowing what her calendar looks like on any given month, I could certainly understand why. Her story needed to be told, and regardless of whether I had a hand in it, I wanted to encourage her to tell the tale.

Enter Thomas Hale, PhD, author of the well-known and well-respected *Medications and Mothers' Milk* reference book and owner of Hale Publishing. He knew Marian and enough of her story to call and ask her to write a memoir which he would publish. And that was why Marian wanted to talk that day, and that's how I ended up with the honor and privilege of helping her write the book you now hold in your hands.

Marian lives in Evanston, Illinois, and I live in rural west Tennessee–500 miles apart. Most of our work on the book was done by phone, with the help of a digital recorder plugged into my phone line. That meant countless hours of recordings to transcribe, picking and choosing the best stories and organizing them into chapters. My husband Bob helped with the transcriptions and enjoyed listening to her stories.

At Marian's suggestion, we added another person to help us–one who had book-writing experience, knew Marian, and had already written a couple of the existing LLL history books–*LLLove Story* and *The Revolutionaries Wore Pearls*. We asked Kaye Lowman Boorom if she would read through the chapters as we drafted them. At first, I was cautiously optimistic about adding this new person to the mix. Marian and Kaye are good friends, but you never know how adding someone to a project will work out. As it turned out, Kaye's insights and encouragement have been invaluable, even when she insisted that some stories just didn't need to be included!

We also asked each of Marian's seven children to send us some memories. All of them sent wonderful tales of growing up in the Tompson household. We've included a few of their stories throughout the book.

While most of the book was done by phone and email, we decided that getting together in person would be worth the time and effort. Once again I enlisted Bob's help–making a 500 mile trip that ended with driving through Chicago during rush hour wasn't anything *I* wanted to do by myself! Bob donned his chauffeur hat, and off we went for the first of two visits to Marian's home.

First impressions are strong and lasting. This applies to people as well as places, and you can tell a lot about a person by the space she inhabits. That first visit to Marian's home in Evanston was a sensory delight. The aroma of homemade chili wafted out to the landing as my husband and I stood at the front door. Greeted with a hug, Marian invited us into her home and her life. Her condo is warm and inviting, and is full of memories and memorabilia of her life as a mother, grandmother, great-grandmother, breastfeeding advocate, and friend. There's the Chinese dog that guards the front door–with two small lizards that appeared to be playfully placed as if nursing. Forget the biology, forget the symbol of protection–what is clear is that breastfeeding and nurturing–and fun–are welcome here.

Scattered around the living room are pictures of family, some as old as Marian's grandparents, some as current as her great-grandchildren, and she delights in introducing her family one by one, picture by picture. We, as the parents of only two children, marvel at her ability to rattle off her seven children's names, those of their respective spouses, where they live, names of their children, and even whether or not they like the picture.

There is a blend of old and new here. Modern furniture has antique quilt squares as accents. "Oh, my daughter Deb got that for me because she knows I love quilts," she comments about one patchwork of predominantly velveteen scraps artfully combined in a two foot square.

An obvious focal point in the room is a large wooden dollhouse, fully decorated inside and out, with everything from a hutch with dishes to a cuckoo clock–and of course, a full house of family members–some by themselves, some "sleeping" in the family bed. Marian laughs, "I figure if I can't keep my own house in order, at least I can keep my dollhouse clean!" Real estate is all about "location, location, location," and the prominent placement of this dollhouse is clearly an invitation to all to come and play–and celebrate the home.

There are those among us who are collectors–be it stamps, porcelain figurines, antiques, you name it. For many, the collection is about the items–"This is a 1946 original Hummel piece." For Marian, it is the memories that are collected, and the pieces are just memory keepers. Each piece tells a story–where she was when she got it, but more importantly, who she met and what that person meant to her.

Marian's life is an eclectic mix: child of the Great Depression, mother of seven, global ambassador of a fledgling breastfeeding support organization, during a time period when most women were either stay-at-home moms or were working as teachers, secretaries, or factory workers. Even when she was speaking at a conference on the other side of the world, her heart–and her priority–was at home, about home, solidly connected to home. For Marian, life begins–and ends–at home, both figuratively and literally. "Home," and all it entails, centers Marian. It inspires her and gives her life purpose.

Marian's home is an eclectic mix of culture and hospitality, of memories of days gone by, and the here and now, all woven together in a warm, inviting tapestry representing an 81 year–and counting–passionate journey through a life unexpected.

Few of us imagine what our lives really hold in store for us–as we look back at where we've come, the path we imagined we might follow years before rarely has our footprints on it. And in the process of looking back, we might be surprised to see the path that our footprints *did* take. Choices, circumstances, historical events, and simple cases of being at the right place at the right time often define our life's roadmap. And yet, what those choices and circumstances *lead to* has more to do with personality and dedication to cause than with random events creating detours in what we believed to be our charted path.

Marian's life is different than she imagined it might be–and the lives she has touched are different from what any of us might have imagined. I wouldn't be writing this introduction to her memoir had it not been for the La Leche

League she helped to found over half a century ago. At least as important as me recharting my own life because of Marian's influence, my current life is truly enriched from this experience, working so closely with a woman I admired long before we met, and with new meaning now that I can count her as a friend.

–Melissa Clark Vickers

April 2011

Beginnings

"You're not going to take my wife into the delivery room unless I go in with her!"

That was my father speaking, as unusual as it was for him to raise his voice. The presence of anybody but the doctor and nurses at a hospital birth was unheard of in 1929.

But this was an unusual situation. My mother had a miscarriage at five months with her first pregnancy, and remembering her devastation at losing the baby, my father stepped in front of the gurney as she was being wheeled down the hall to the delivery room. He knew he had to stay with her in case something else went wrong this time.

And so I was born on December 5, 1929, at 4:50 a.m., in Ravenswood Hospital in Chicago: my mother, a bit woozy because of the ether cone put over her face during her last contraction, and my father, awake and alert at her side, to protect his wife and greet his daughter.

It was an unexpected turn on a commonplace event and set the stage for a life I could never have anticipated.

Family Matters

If my grandparents had anything to do with it, my parents probably never would have married.

It didn't matter that my mother's father was a respected sculptor who had won medals in Tuscany for his art work and had been brought to Chicago by a statuary company in 1901, along with his wife and two older children. (My mother and three more siblings would be born in the United States.) Never mind that my father's father owned a dairy farm that was run by tenant farmers while he lived in the city and was so successful that he was able to retire in his 30's.

The problem was an ethnic one. Dad's heritage was Irish, English, and Scotch. My mother was Italian.

Each family thought their precious child was marrying "down." Luckily, love won out, bringing me grandparents who had lasting effects on my life, starting with Marianne, my maternal grandmother, after whom I was named.

At the time I was born, at least in the United States, it was common to tell mothers that to prevent "spoiling" their babies, they were only to be picked up every four hours, when it was time to feed them by breast or bottle. My mother's friends told me of the heartbreak of listening to the baby cry as they kept an eye on the clock, waiting for permission to pick up and feed the baby. But my grandmother, Marianne, said babies were not meant to cry, so I was held and fed as needed. The Chicago Public Health Department recommended that breastfeeding mothers drink a quart of milk a day! My mother later strongly suspected the colic I suffered with then, and the milk sensitivity I have to this day, came from all that milk, which, incidentally, was something she never drank growing up in her Italian household.

Here I am at 2, feeling right at home in the rocking chair

But having colic meant I got a lot of holding, and it was probably out of desperation that I slept in the same bed with my parents for the first year of my life. Keeping me within easy reach at night might have been their only chance of getting some sleep! I was 50 years old before my mother admitted this, and I figured that parents were given so many threats about the psychological damage that could be done to babies when sleeping with an adult that my mother waited to see how I turned out before she told me about our family bed.

My father held a variety of jobs during his life. He didn't care to have a boss breathing down his neck, so he worked as a lineman, climbing telephone poles to string phone lines; managed a gas station; was a motorman on the streetcars; and later became a milk man delivering milk to homes, as was the custom in those days. When my mother came into some money after the death of a relative in Italy, my father was able to buy his own milk route, which he ran until his death at 62. Although he was the only one of his family who did not graduate from college, his three siblings often described him as the happiest member of the family.

My mother had expected to go to college. She was enrolled at Northwestern University in Evanston, where I live now. She toured the campus with her father, and hoped to become a kindergarten teacher. But her mother's advancing rheumatoid arthritis and the need for her to stay home to take care of her mother, the house, and her younger siblings prevented her from ever realizing that dream. While she always thought that people who went to college were smarter than she was, she had more life skills than most people and was my constant source of helpful information until the day she died at 84.

I wasn't an only child for long. Just after my second birthday, my sister Esther came along, and then Adrienne, followed by the "baby," Charles. We were probably a pretty typical middle-class family. Still affected by the depression, money was always tight, but we never felt deprived. My mother was a wonder at stretching what little money we had. She sewed all the girls' clothes–my first piece of store-bought clothing was a suit my aunts bought me when I graduated from grammar school. Mom was a natural cook, baked her own bread, and when dinner was an Italian dish my father didn't particularly like, she cooked a separate meal for him. Saturday night dinner was "leftover" night. She would make a pie crust, and then mix up all the finely cut up vegetables and meat left over from meals during the week, stir in some eggs, and bake it. I didn't especially appreciate it then, but it seems like a tasty idea now.

My parents, sister Esther, and me

We lived in a variety of apartments and flats as I was growing up. I don't know if it was because of finances or my grandmother's arthritis, but for a few years, during which my sister Adrienne was born, we lived with my grandparents, with our family sleeping in one big bedroom.

My grandmother's arthritis kept her confined to a room on the second floor where she sat in a comfortable chair beside a window reading the books that were picked up for her at the library each week. On Saturday afternoons, my grandparents listened to the opera on the radio, and in an early form of karaoke, my grandmother often sang along with the women's parts, while my grandfather, in another part of the house, sang the men's parts. Through the ears of a young child, they sounded wonderful!

I was five years old and living in my grandparents' house when I got my first and only spanking. Every family makes their own decisions about the use of certain words and phrases. As strange as it might seem today, in our family using the word "gut" or the phrase "son of a gun" were grounds for a spanking. One day, playing out in the back yard with friends from the neighborhood, my sister Esther did something (which for the life of me I can't recall) that made me so angry I wanted to hit her. But I was bigger and older than Esther. I remember feeling that hitting her wouldn't be fair, so I did the next worst thing and called her a "son of a gun." I didn't notice that she went straight into the house to tell my mother, so I was surprised when my mother called me into the kitchen, my little friends trailing behind me. Mother sat down in a chair, put me over her lap, and spanked me right in front of my friends! I learned my lesson and never got another spanking. Nor did I feel the need to use spanking to discipline my children when I became a mother. Guess I was a quick study!

Another house that carries special memories during my later grammar school and high school years was a large wooden house that had been turned into a two-flat. It is still across the street from the three-flat brick house owned by my dad's parents, where my dad was born and our family lived for a time. The large wooden house had been owned by the then-imprisoned physician who removed the fingerprints of John Dillinger, the famous criminal. Dillinger had been shot and killed coming out of the Biograph movie theater a few blocks away. The Biograph was where we went to see movies for 15 cents on Saturday afternoons.

During most of my childhood, we lived within walking distance of Lincoln Park. This meant we went to the park often and felt like it was an extension of our back yard. During one period when my father worked nights and slept each morning, my mother would walk us, my cousins, and other children from the neighborhood to North Avenue Beach on Lake Michigan, so my dad could sleep undisturbed. We would stay at the beach all morning, playing in the water, and then walk back through the park and be home in time for lunch. I never heard my mother complain about this interruption of her day, and I'm so grateful for the fun we had. It wasn't until years later that my mother realized that my father could sleep through any kind of noise, so those trips to the beach were probably not necessary, but they added so much to my wonderful childhood memories.

Mother always cared about the people in her life, and she was a born organizer. When we moved to the suburbs, an unincorporated area with unpaved streets, the neighbors said she brought the neighborhood together. There was a standing invitation to our home on Friday nights. We had a piano and Myrtle, from across the street, would play the piano while we all sang. This was back in the time when neighborhoods were real communities, and neighbors provided much needed social connections–long before the advent of "social networking" via email, Facebook, or texting.

My mother did every kind of handwork, and in her later years until she died, she had weekly gatherings at her house of women whose ages ranged from the 20s to the 80s. They brought whatever handwork they were working on and might need help with, and discussed what was going on in the world as they worked. They called themselves "The Happy Hookers," thoroughly enjoying the double meaning of the group's name.

As my sisters and I got married, we had a standing invitation for Sunday dinners at my parents' house. (Sometimes attending a dinner we didn't have to pay for was the only way we could financially make it through the week.) As our families grew and more room was needed, my mother had an addition built across the entire back of the house, with a large table that held all of us at least for a while. Later, the grandchildren were moved to a table in the dining room, which led to much merriment emanating from the "children's table," as you might suspect.

It's true that we are influenced in some way by everyone who touches our life, but nobody as strongly as our mothers. I'm still influenced by my mother's generosity, much as she was influenced by her mother, who it was said never turned away anyone asking for help, whether it was a neighbor in need or a panhandler looking for a meal.

So this, briefly told, was the foundation for my life. I had great teachers and much good fortune from the very beginning. My formal schooling, just ahead, would bring with it surprises, a lot of changes, and new interests.

School Days

By the time I finished my formal education in 12th grade, I was 17 years old, and except for kindergarten and my senior year, all my learning had taken place in Catholic schools.

You got a good education in Catholic schools. The fact that many of us were afraid of the nuns back then probably helped. You did what you were told, and if there was a problem, you could count on your parents standing up for your teacher. In hindsight, it wouldn't surprise me if the nuns were a little scared of us, too. A classroom with 50 students could be intimidating. In desperation to keep order, the nuns often resorted to approaches that might not be acceptable today.

Sister Mary B, my second grade teacher, was a case in point. I had only been in first grade a short while when, to my surprise, I was promoted to second grade. The fact that I already knew how to read might have been the reason, but when I walked into the second grade classroom, Sister Mary B was busy teaching and told me to stand in front of the room beside her desk until she had time to get me settled in. So I stood there with my little armful of supplies and got a firsthand look at her unique system for keeping order.

It was quite simple really. Tiny and soon to celebrate her 50th year as a nun, Sister had a bunch of balls on the floor beside her desk. When she noticed someone talking or misbehaving, she would pick up a ball and throw it at that child. Of course, the guilty person usually knew this might happen, so he would be on the lookout, ready to duck, leaving some poor innocent child sitting behind to get hit with the ball. But not to worry! The child who was hit by mistake was then given the remarkable opportunity of standing in front of the class ready to throw a ball at the next student who misbehaved. This was my introduction to second grade.

Of course, I didn't know what the rules were for second grade–these were seasoned kids–and I was definitely an outsider. Then, one day at recess, a girl came up to me and said, "My name is Marie and I'll be your friend." What a difference that made, having a friend who explained what was going on and who made me feel like part of the group. Hmmm, the importance of information and support–was I learning an even bigger lesson here?

During my short time in first grade, though, I was told that writing with my left hand was not acceptable. It smeared the paper. So using my right hand became a challenge that actually affects my perception even today. If you want to stop me cold when I am driving my car, just ask me to *turn left right here*.

Apparently, turning lefties into righties was not an uncommon practice, even though I was quick to blame the change when unable to make a quick decision. Many years later, my mother accompanied me to India for a Pediatric Conference where I had been invited to speak. Visiting a home where Gandhi once lived, we learned that as a child he, too, had been required to change to writing with his right hand instead of his left. "Marian, if Gandhi could make something of himself despite changing hands, so can you," my mother teased.

Music was always part of my schooling. In order to pay for piano lessons, my sister Esther and I cleaned the parlors in the convent where the nuns lived. On Sunday afternoons, I also helped prepare dinner for the nuns. The irony was that while I was doing all this extra work to take music lessons, I was petrified by the piano teacher. Walking to school for my lesson, I sometimes thought that getting hit by a car as I stepped off the curb would be preferable to having to face Sister Mary J's authoritarian style.

Next came violin lessons with a borrowed violin. My mother was more worried about the neighbors downstairs having to live with the sound of me practicing than she was about my progress. But I continued playing violin through high school in the school orchestras. I loved being swept up in the sound of all of us playing together. Within two years of leaving high school, I was married and having babies, and playing the violin disappeared from my life. But it had served its purpose to help me understand and enjoy music, and my life moved on.

I went to three different high schools. I received a one-year scholarship to Holy Name Cathedral High School in Chicago upon graduation from eighth grade, so that's where I spent my freshman year. But since most of my girlfriends were going to Immaculata, an all girls' high school on the north side of Chicago, my parents finally gave in and allowed me to switch to Immaculata for my sophomore and junior years.

Immaculata was a much more upscale school. Unlike Holy Name Cathedral where you sat and ate your bagged lunch in the gym, Immaculata had an actual school cafeteria and a school paper. I worked in the cafeteria to help with my tuition and joined the newspaper staff, introducing a new column, "Did You Know," in which I presented what I thought was interesting information about the school and the students. How many lefties vs. righties? Chocolate milk vs. white milk? Favorite books and movies? It was my introduction to research and data collection.

Our lives changed substantially at the end of my junior year. My dad always loved horses, and we moved out of Chicago to accommodate the horses that had become part of our family. One of my earliest memories as a toddler was sitting on the grass with my mother, watching Dad play polo. I couldn't have been more than five years old when he started taking me horseback riding at a stable in the suburbs. Although I was short for my age, he insisted that I always ride a horse, never a pony. So it was an exciting event in our family when my father bought Sandy, an English riding horse, from his boss at Bowman Dairy, and later, Joe, a quarter horse. Now my mother and father could ride together. Money was never discussed in our family, and to this day we don't know how Dad was able to afford two horses. He must have gotten a bargain!

As teenagers, Esther and I were allowed to ride the horses down to Lincoln Park by ourselves. Looking back as adults, we are amazed that our parents allowed us to do this. But it was a safer time, with much less traffic, and we never had a problem.

I'm riding Sandy, and my cousin Marie is on Joe on our way to Lincoln Park

The horses were originally stabled a few blocks from our house, but after awhile, and probably to save money, my parents decided to look for a house west of the Chicago city limits where we could keep Sandy and Joe on our own property. They rode the streetcar to the end of the line, found a real estate office, and ended up buying a small two-story house on an acre of land for $4700. This was 1946, and the house was in an unincorporated area of Melrose Park.

The move meant Esther and I could no longer go to Immaculata. There just was no good way of getting there using public transportation. So we enrolled in the local public high school, Leyden High School in Franklin Park. Leyden was just three miles from our house, but it could have been in another universe from what it was like growing up in Chicago Catholic schools.

At Immaculata, when you walked through the halls from one class to another, there was total silence. Nobody talked, and the nuns stood outside their classrooms to make sure you didn't. In contrast, at Leyden the sound could be deafening with everyone talking and laughing. There were quick kisses and even hair spray being applied as students changed classes—it was noisy, but fun. In Catholic school, when the teacher asked a question, you raised your hand and waited to be acknowledged. Then you'd stand up and give your answer. At Leyden, in contrast, the teacher would ask a question and before I could raise my hand, three other students had already shouted out the answer from their seats. It took me a while to get with this new protocol.

I was never the most popular girl in class. I was very shy. But when acting in plays, even in grammar school, I could hide my shyness. I liked giving the impression of a girl who was quick-witted and not tongue-tied, especially if there were boys in the audience. I remember playing Katherine in a shortened version of *The Taming of the Shrew* at Leyden. I wore a beautiful Elizabethan costume that made me feel very Shakespearean. After the play the principal said to me, "I *knew* you could get mad! You are always so nice!"

In the Leyden High School yearbook, the description under my picture reads: "Wants to either be a lab technician or a Pavlova." Reflected in that statement was a bit of prophecy and passion. Being a lab technician meant "research" to me, and I actually couldn't understand why that appealed to me at the time. My image of doing research was looking through a microscope all day, and it sounded so boring! Ballet, however–now *that* was understandable. *That* was my passion, but not my fate.

My high school graduation picture, in 1947

3

A Foot Like Pavlova's

Fifteen years old is a bit old to start ballet lessons. The great Russian ballerina Anna Pavlova was dancing before she was ten. Pavlova fell in love with ballet after she attended a performance of *Sleeping Beauty*. I saw my first ballet, *Les Sylphides*, at 15, and that's when I fell in love with dancing!

My parents couldn't afford to pay for ballet lessons, so Nonno, my mother's father, who had been living with us since my grandmother's death in 1940, agreed to pay for them. My first teacher, in the Fine Arts Building in downtown Chicago, was Belle Bender. She had an ad for her classes in the *Les Sylphides* dance program. After my first class, she said she found it hard to believe that I'd never studied ballet before. It seemed, at least as a beginner, that I was a natural.

After a while, my new friend from class, Pat, and I decided to check out some of the other teachers in town, and after observing a number of classes, settled on the Stone-Camryn School of Ballet. Walter Camryn and Bentley Stone were well known in the ballet world as teachers, dancers, and choreographers, and were particularly successful at placing their graduates in professional companies.

After graduating from high school, I was hired as a receptionist for an architectural firm in downtown Chicago. I'd take the train into the city each morning, and at least three or four nights a week after work, I'd head to ballet class a few blocks away. Compliments from my teachers had to be earned, but I was told that I had a foot like Pavlova's. I don't know if it made me a better dancer, but the thought did help carry me through the intense workouts.

It was particularly exciting when professional ballet troupes came to town because some of the dancers would always join in our classes, and occasionally students would be enlisted for crowd scenes in the ballets.

When Ballet Russe de Monte Carlo, the famous Russian ballet troupe, came to Chicago to perform *Petrouchka,* I got to be in it. This was my dream! What a treat to be dressed in costume and hang about back stage with the dancers! I never spent the dollar bill each of us received as payment, but encased it in plastic along with some of the confetti that was thrown about in the crowd scene.

Several of my ballet classmates went on to fame and fortune in movies and theater. Janice Rule and I used to run through dark, empty streets downtown after class to catch our trains to go home. Chicago was safer then! Janice suggested I audition with her for *High Button Shoes*, a musical that was on tour in Chicago. It was tempting, but by that time, I had met the man who would take my life in yet another direction. So Janice went on to roles on the stage as a dancer, and then as an actor onstage with Paul Newman in *Picnic,* and later in films. She then became a psychoanalyst, and after a while, we lost touch.

Leslie Browne, who won an Oscar for Best Actress in a Supporting Role in the 1977 film, *The Turning Point*, was the daughter of Kelly Browne, a regular in class until he left for Hollywood films. Kelly was always fun to watch, and he and his wife would be in class whenever they were in town.

I loved dancing. I loved it so much that after I made the decision to give it up, I found, to my surprise, that I could not watch a ballet or a movie about dance for years. I willingly made the decision to give up dancing, and I knew without a doubt that it was the right decision, but even so, it hurt so much to just sit and watch, but not be able to dance. If dancing is in your blood, it is hard to give it up. It would be one of many decisions I made over the years that I didn't really grasp the significance of until much later, but this one ultimately led to marriage, children, La Leche League, and a life I could never have imagined. Luckily, Tom, my intended, grew to love ballroom dancing as we went to the many weddings of family and friends. Take me dancing and I'm yours!

I did return to ballet classes for a little while after my first two children were born. It surprised Mr. Camryn–and me–that my technique was better than ever, despite not having time to practice after getting married and starting a family. My teachers said my dancing reflected more maturity, and so they refunded the money left over from when I quit lessons earlier in order to encourage me to continue. "We never give money back to people, but you are doing so well!" they said. But within months I was pregnant with my third baby. Fate was calling me back home–just as it had come calling a few years earlier *and* led me to Tom, while on a quest for a motorcycle.

I still have my toe shoes somewhere, packed in a box. Tom wanted to bronze them, but I thought that was a bit ostentatious. Those shoes are packed away with the reminder of a different path my life might have taken–if not for the love of a good man.

Mom was a ballerina when she was younger. I loved holding her ballet slippers and putting on her toe shoes, trying to walk around the house. I always thought of her as a beautiful princess in a leotard and tutu, with her hair pulled up and a tiara on her head. She most definitely has the panache to pull it off!

As a little girl, it was like having a fairy princess for my mother, knowing she had been a ballerina. I took dance lessons from her friend and wanted to be just like my mom. The very special memory I have, though, is when I was a teen and took ballet lessons, and my mother took them with me.

How beautiful to see the person I saw in this "box" of responsibility, who cooked, cleaned, and drove me places, gracefully leaping into the air across the floor, so precisely, yet elegantly mastering the positions! I have never seen a picture of my mother when she was a ballerina, but I had the honor of seeing her dance!

–Sheila Tompson Doucet

4

"I Wish for Shining Moments"

As a teen in high school, I wasn't counting the days until I got married and had babies. I didn't spend time daydreaming about walking down the aisle on my wedding day. My life was busy with work, ballet classes, and community theatre. All those other things would happen in their own good time. Of course, once married I would stay home as a wife and mother whose life revolved around her home and family. As it turned out, I *did* become a wife and mother, and my life *did* revolve around home and family, but with an added dimension I couldn't have imagined at 16.

We had moved to the unincorporated Melrose Park area outside Chicago, so we could house the horses my father bought on our own property. It was my last year of high school, and my first year since kindergarten that I attended public school. I had become friends with Nick, my ballet friend Pat's brother, and Nick wanted to buy a motorcycle. He heard that with World War II being over you could purchase Harley Davidson "Army bikes" cheaply. I remembered seeing two men on khaki-colored motorcycles riding the unpaved road in front of our house. So I told Nick that I would find out where the men lived and see what I could find out about those motorcycles, which came folded in a box and sold for $100.

I wasn't about to go to a strange house alone, so my sister Adrienne walked with me down the road to the rustic English style tri-level house known in the neighborhood as "Hobby House." Built entirely by Ken Wiggins, a musician, sportsman, and artist, to house his hobbies, it contained a pipe organ in the two-story living room and what looked like the beginning of a free form pool in the front yard. Adrienne and I introduced ourselves to a man standing in the front yard who turned out to be Ken. Then Ken said, "I'd like you to meet Tommy," as he pointed to a hole in the ground. We waited for a few minutes until Tom, who was hooking up the pump for the swimming pool and covered with dirt, climbed out of the hole.

Tom had been in the Army signal corps from the beginning of World War II until it ended. He met Ken while they were both soldiers. Instead of going home to New England after the war, where jobs were not easy to find, Tom decided to look for work in Chicago. He lived in a Chicago YMCA for awhile, and then got a job at Zenith. Ken, who also worked at Zenith, invited Tom to live with him in Hobby House, right down the street from me! Adrienne and I didn't stay long that first time, but we got the information we came for.

Apparently, we weren't the only ones who had gotten information from that chance meeting–Tom later told me that when he climbed out of the hole and saw me, he knew that one day, when I was old enough, he would ask me to marry him. I, on the other hand, had no inkling that he was *the one*.

Tom looking dapper in 1948

As soon as I graduated from high school, Tom quickly began subtly "courting me," dropping by the house. Our first "date" was a drive to Riverview, the famous Chicago amusement park, with Adrienne and Ken. Within a few months, Tom had taken me to two musicals, the opera, and the ballet. He introduced me to frog legs, subgum chow mein, scallops, and shrimp cocktails. I'd played my first slot machine and taken an airplane ride in a Piper Cub. Tom gave me record albums of music from ballets and musicals, and had taken me to eat at a dozen restaurants. My world had gotten significantly larger in just a few months!

Tom was not only fun to be with–he had a dry sense of humor that always made me laugh, he also enjoyed just sitting and talking. Our conversations were so much more interesting than those I had with the boys from high school. But I still wasn't thinking about marriage. Before long, Tom started driving downtown after he finished work to pick me up from ballet class. In the summer, he would bring along a gallon jug of freshly made ice cold lemonade and we'd go over to Grant Park, sit on the grass, and listen to music at the Bandshell. One day, in an effort to impress me, he asked to ride Joe, the quarter horse. He showed up wearing regular shoes and trousers, climbed on Joe, and Joe, responding as quarter horses do, took off down the road–fast! Tom held on for dear life, so tightly that by the time he managed to return, blood from chafing on the inside of his legs was dripping down into his shoes. He never said a word about his condition. Just coolly got off the horse and walked home.

———

Tom was born in New Hampshire. He was the middle child of three boys, and his parents divorced when he was three years old. The problems that led to the divorce were never discussed, but his mother's Catholic family was outraged that she would take that step. So when she asked them for help caring for the boys during the day while she went to work to support them, the family refused. Her only alternative was to put them in a local Catholic orphanage run by French nuns. The boys went in, not understanding a word of what was said to them in French. They came out three years later speaking French in an English speaking world. It is heartbreaking even now to think of what it must have been like for Tom, his brothers, and his mother. Tom's mother visited them on weekends, and the boys would stand by the front door crying when she left. She was able to take the boys out of the orphanage when she married Edwin Tompson, a railroad man. She had been breastfeeding her youngest son, Al, when they went into the orphanage, and the day she got them back home one of the first things she did was to take Al into the bedroom to see if he still wanted to nurse. He didn't.

Ed, as he was called, legally adopted the boys, and the brothers always referred to him as their dad. My children loved Grandpa Tompson, and he lived with us for awhile after Tom's mother died. Tom's given name was actually Clement, but people called him Tom because of his new last name–Tom Tompson.

Tom was a real romantic and a very sentimental man. We constantly wrote notes to each other both before and after we were married. After a date we would each write a note, and then exchange them when we got together again. He gave me a charm bracelet that memorialized many of those special occasions.

Tom proposed marriage at dinner at a fancy French restaurant in Chicago. As was usual in those days, he did ask permission of my parents first. My mother said that of all my boyfriends (and I really didn't have that many) she felt that Tom and I were the best suited to be together. So I was prepared for a proposal when we went to dinner that night and immediately said "Yes!"

Not only did I want to marry Tom, I had to! Still very much on my mind was the talk on sex that Father J gave to the juniors at Immaculata High School only two years earlier. While I don't remember anything about the talk, it was Father's response to a question asked later by a student that stuck in my mind.

"Father, what is a French kiss?" the brave girl asked. "That's a kiss between two French people," Father helpfully explained, but then he added, with stern emphasis, "Remember, you never kiss a boy with more passion than you would kiss a doorknob unless you are going to get married."

And Tom just wouldn't stop kissing me!

On May 7, 1949, I became Mrs. Clement Ralph Tompson. As I look back over my life, I believe that Tom and I were *intended* to meet, fall in love, and marry. My life would never have turned out the way it did with another man. Tom later told me that when we met he realized that I was an independent thinker and needed my freedom. I was so surprised that he saw that in me. I always thought of myself as a quiet, obedient person— that first born child who had to set a good example for the children who followed. Maybe it was because he was eleven years older, but Tom not only saw that need, he was also willing to give me the freedom, along with any support and encouragement I needed. It was largely because he was so much older than me that I decided to give up the ballet I so dearly loved. I didn't think it was fair to him to have to wait any longer to have a family once we were married. As hard as that decision was, marrying Tom couldn't have been more right for me and where my life would lead.

Leaving for my wedding, May 7, 1949

Our wedding took place in St. Gertrude's Church in Franklin Park. My father had just bought a new car, and in those days you were not supposed to drive very fast while breaking the car in. He drove so slowly to the church I was afraid we would be late! But we got there in time for the wedding ceremony and Mass. I carried a bouquet of white lilacs and was bursting with teenage joy as my father proudly walked me down the aisle. Tom, on the other hand, the only adult in this twosome, looks rather nervous in some of our wedding pictures.

Presenting Mr. and Mrs. Clement Ralph Tompson!

Our reception was lunch at a local restaurant that was closed to the public for the occasion. We had a fried chicken dinner for about a hundred wedding guests.

"Take me dancing, and I'm yours!"

For our honeymoon, Tom took two weeks off work, and we drove to Estes Park, Colorado, and the Rocky Mountain National Park. This trip was a big deal for me. I had never been west of the Mississippi River before, had never seen a mountain, and had never been away from my family. And I'd certainly never been a newlywed! Tom liked to be spontaneous, so right after the reception, we changed clothes, put our suitcases in the car, and just started driving. As it got late, we were hard put to find a cabin or hotel where we would spend our first night as husband and wife. The motel we finally found was quite rundown. It had two rooms and Tom took both of them, for a total of $4.00, so we could have some privacy. When we awoke the next morning, there was a horse with his head stuck in our window.

One of the very few pictures that turned out from our honeymoon

We drove down the famous Route 66, stopping many times to take pictures with the 35 mm camera Tom had borrowed from a friend. My first glimpse of the mountains ahead was exciting, but driving through them was scary. I didn't have a driver's license, so Tom did the driving, and he wasn't fazed by two lane highways with drop-offs to infinity. I tried to help by leaning in toward the mountains so as not to tip the car over the edge. But we met our match going up one mountain when we were stopped by a wooden barrier across the road with a sign stating that because of the snow, the road was closed. "Why wasn't that sign posted at the bottom of the mountain?" I asked. Now Tom had to turn the car around on the narrow, two lane, icy road, with no railing to prevent a plunge. Well, it took me less than a minute to decide that as Tom's wife it was my duty to get out of the car immediately so if there was an accident while he turned the car around, I could walk back down the mountain to get help, knowing exactly where our car had left the road! The turnaround was successful, and when we arrived at Estes Park, we rented a cabin for the next four nights, spending our days hiking in the mountains looking for deer and elk. A ranger we met on the trail gave us a large elk antler he had found. We were thrilled, but 61 years later, I still don't know what to do with it! Tom, I have to admit, cooked most of our meals on our honeymoon. As a bachelor, he was much more experienced at cooking than I was, and he enjoyed doing it. And I enjoyed letting him! He was a good cook, and it was nice to be pampered.

———

When we got back from our two-week honeymoon, we had spent a total of $228.15! This covered everything–our gas, food, the cabins we stayed in with prices that ranged from $2.00 to $6.00 a night, 20 cents for Tom's occasional pack of cigarettes, postcards, and souvenirs. Tom was very good at keeping track of expenses, and we didn't have a lot of money to spend. But when we got the rolls of film developed, only a handful of the photographs were any good, out of the dozens of pictures we took. We never figured out what went wrong with the camera, but we always had our memories!

Our honeymoon had wiped out our savings account, so we had little money to spend by the time Christmas came around that first year. After we bought gifts for the family, Tom and I were left with a total of one dollar each to buy gifts for each other. Tom didn't have a watch at the time, and my grandfather had an old wrist watch with a broken band on it that he wasn't using. So Nonno gave me that watch for Tom, and I bought a replacement band with the dollar. Tom knew I loved to read and found a book club that you could join for a dollar and get three free books. I still have one of those books, *The City in the Dawn*, by Hervey Allen. Tom's inscription, hinting at things to come, says "A key to new worlds from your loving husband."

Tom was working for Zenith as an electro-mechanical engineer at the time we were married, and he continued to work there for over 25 years in a variety of positions, ending up with product development. He got patents for a number of components in Zenith television sets. Problems needing to be solved were always tucked in his head, even when he was engaged in something else. For a while Zenith had a lighted knob on its TV set, where the number of the channel lit up as you turned the knob. That was one of Tom's inventions. His solution for making that knob came one evening when we were sitting at the dinner table talking about other things, and he suddenly said, "I've got it!" He jumped up from the table, brought back a piece of paper and pencil, and drew the knob as it should be built. I had such confidence in Tom's ability to fix anything that I used to say if someone popped a balloon he would find a way to put it back together.

Tom liked to cut out poems by James J. Metcalfe from the daily paper and give them to me when we were dating. He knew I loved poetry. Later, he put more of these poems in a little notebook for my birthday that I treasure to this day. I know that today, emails and text messages are often used to send messages to those we love, but somehow, having a handwritten note beats a typed note on the computer screen hands down.

And who sends telegrams today? Little compares to the thrill of receiving a special anniversary message delivered by Western Union:

I wish for shining moments to fill this happy day STOP May gifts of love and friendship be scattered along your way STOP May this day bring real contentment and new day's joy and peace and may every happiness be yours in life and for evermore increase STOP Happy anniversary, from Tommy.

5

"Doctor, How Did You Do It?"

It goes without saying that life in 1949 when I was a newlywed was very different than it is today. Some of the most striking differences for women between these two time periods revolved around birth control and birth options. As a Catholic, birth control was not even open for discussion and that was fine with me. Having read and been beguiled by the book, *Cheaper by the Dozen* by Frank Gibreth, Jr., I wanted a large family. Tom, the middle of three boys, had grown up thinking there was something mentally unstable in anyone choosing to have more than three children. Fortunately for us, the birth of Melanie, our first child, made him a convert to fatherhood, and he genuinely welcomed all subsequent additions to our family.

No one ever talked about pregnancy and fertility cycles in those days, so it was a surprise to discover a few weeks after our wedding that I was pregnant with a honeymoon baby. In retrospect I appreciated that as Catholics we were freed from making all those decisions couples have to agree on today before having a baby. "Can we afford a baby and the cost of educating it?" "When should it be born so that I can take time off from work?" "I'm a teacher, so can we time the birth for summer vacation?" And then you had to actually *get* pregnant when you decided the time was right. Tom and I didn't have those concerns. And though we were living from paycheck to paycheck, whether or not we could afford another baby was never an issue. It might sound irresponsible today, but we just left it up to God and felt God would provide. I used to joke, "Tom just had to walk in the door and I'd be pregnant!"

After we were married, Tom and I moved in with his friend Ken, just down the street from my parents. For $10 a week, we rented a tiny bedroom on the second floor. The room had no closet, so we hung our clothes on the side of the steps going up to the attic that was accessed from our room. A tiny crib for the baby barely fit. In order to open the attic door to get to our clothes, we had to take the crib out into the hall. We used to talk about having my uncle Ralph, an architect, build us a home that Tom designed. It didn't ever happen. We never had enough money to build our own home. We built a family instead.

As little control as we seemed to have at the time as far as getting pregnant went, it paled in comparison to the lack of control a woman had during the typical labor and delivery in 1950. Had it not been for my serendipitous discovery of an article about Dr. Grantly Dick-Read in the *Ladies Home Journal* while I was still in high school, I probably would have had one of those typical hospital deliveries–knocked out and unaware of what was going on. Instead, I wanted an unmedicated, natural childbirth, convinced that it was doable and the safest way to have a baby.

You didn't "doctor shop" in those days. I went to Dr. O, my aunt Bernie's obstetrician. In total naiveté, I told Dr. O that I wanted to have a natural birth and that I had purchased a copy of Dr. Dick-Read's book, *Childbirth Without Fear*. Dr. O's usual practice was to use what was called "twilight sleep," where a woman sometimes didn't wake up until the next day. He had never seen a "natural childbirth," but he amazingly agreed to go along with me. Although he hadn't read *Childbirth Without Fear*, he told me to do whatever the book said in preparation for the birth. He would let me have my baby without drugs or anesthetics. And, do you know? He actually did! In fact he did more than that. When I needed it, he gave me the confidence that I *could* do it.

My father had asked me not to tell my mother when I went into labor because she would just start worrying. So, of course, Tom and I went to the hospital much too soon. If I had been able to talk to her, I'm sure my mother would have suggested waiting before going to the hospital. As it turned out, we were a whole day early. Walking into the hospital, it hit me. There was no backing out of the delivery awaiting me, no postponing for a day when I might feel more rested–or more capable. It was a "growing up" moment.

But during labor, because I was awake, I became acutely aware of how unsuitable a place the hospital was to have a baby, and how clueless most birth attendants were to the needs of the woman in labor.

First of all, no one expressed any excitement that I was about to have a baby! I could have been there for an appendectomy! When she learned I was going to have an unmedicated birth, one nurse tried to convince me that the Read

Method of Natural Childbirth was fine in theory, but wouldn't work once I got in the delivery room. How I would have appreciated having someone with me who understood what I was going through to help me have the birth experience I wanted.

Husbands were assumed to be superfluous and might even get in the way of hospital procedure, so Tom wasn't encouraged to stay with me. There were two beds in the small labor room, which was right next to the delivery room. When both beds were occupied, only one husband was allowed in the room at a time. If someone was in the delivery room next door, neither husband could be in the labor room. And, of course, husbands were NOT allowed in the delivery room at all.

As evening approached, a nurse told Tom it was time for him to go home. And he did—most people were pretty obedient in those days to authority figures, and few people were more authoritative than doctors and nurses. My bed was right by the window, and it was the most desolate feeling watching Tom walk away down the dark street. I had felt that as long as he was there, he would protect me. And now he was gone! Almost as soon as Tom got home, though, he asked himself, "What am I doing here?" and came back to the hospital. But he still wasn't allowed in the room with me. That's what the father's waiting room was for.

Listening to what was going on in the delivery room next door was frightening. The women, who were all drugged, were either moaning or screaming. And then I would hear somebody say something like, "If you don't be quiet I'm going to walk out of this room and leave you." I had *never* heard one adult speak to another adult with such disdain before in my life.

"It's bedtime," the nurse said, as she came into the labor room and turned off the lights. Was I supposed to go to sleep just because she put the lights out? How do I go to sleep while I'm in *labor*? Being the first planned natural birth in a hospital wasn't easy—especially when the staff had no idea what it was like for an awake and unmedicated mother.

But my saving grace in the middle of the night was Dr. O. He was in the hospital for another delivery, and he came into my room and said, "Marian, if you can handle whatever you're feeling right now, then you can make it all the way through." That's all I needed. When he said that, I was able to relax completely between contractions during the hours still ahead. This was the middle of the night, and my baby wasn't born until the middle of the next morning. Dr. O's assurance that my body would be able to deliver my baby in the way it was designed to do was all I needed to carry me through the rest of my labor.

I labored for 36 hours. The reason for this long labor, I was later told, was because of a posterior presentation. My baby was face up in the birth canal, rather than face down, making it much more difficult for the baby's neck to bend and slip through the canal. When I was finally taken into the delivery room the next morning, Dr. O said "You know, Marian, if you were knocked out, I would use forceps to get the baby out." And I thought, this would have been done without asking me because I would have been unconscious. "I've heard that forceps aren't good for the baby," I commented. And he said, "Well, it depends on who's using them." But I said, "No. Thank you." Imagine that–shy Marian Leonard Tompson told that *doctor* "no!"–and he listened! Clearly, there was more to this transformation from woman to mother; I was *empowered.*

Then, without thinking, a nurse threw a sheet over my head–*over my head!* Since women were knocked out for delivery, they were used to just concentrating on the other end. I objected and they took the sheet off. My wrists were strapped to the delivery table–another bizarre custom of the day. All the while, the nurses and doctor chatted about their dreams and their dates. Obviously, they weren't used to talking to the mother or having the mother listen in on their conversations. As the baby was being born though, a nurse angled an overhead mirror so I could see the baby emerge.

What a moment that was! The baby emerged looking like an inanimate doll. Then suddenly, she took a breath and started crying, and she was a real live baby! It was one of the most thrilling moments of my life. February 7, 1950: Welcome to the world, Melanie Tompson!

When the nurse gave me a shot to eject the placenta, I said, "Ouch!" "Oh, you were so quiet during the birth, I didn't think you could feel anything!" she responded.

Of course, I wasn't allowed to touch Melanie nor could I with my wrists still strapped to the delivery table. Melanie was whisked to the nursery, and I was taken to my room.

I had no sooner gotten into bed when a nun, accompanied by a young nurse, came in. Sister was holding a copy of that week's issue of *Life* magazine in her hands. She plopped the magazine with a cover story on natural childbirth on my belly and said to the nurse, "This is what this woman just had, a natural childbirth!"

You stayed in the hospital for four days after giving birth in those days. And that meant the hospital would be the setting for the next step of my plan to do the natural thing. I wanted to breastfeed.

Just as I was convinced about the importance of an unmedicated childbirth, it made sense to me that breastfeeding was the way to go, too, even though my *Better Homes and Gardens* baby book said that it made no difference if a baby was breastfed or formula-fed. Nobody tried to talk me into breastfeeding. It just seemed that intuitively–or intelligently–that it would be the best way to nourish my baby.

I wasn't given Melanie to nurse until the next day. When my milk came in, my breasts got so hard I thought they would rip right open. That made any attempt by Melanie to latch on correctly impossible, and so my nipples were in rough shape. Dr. O, who apparently didn't have many breastfeeding mothers in his practice, recommended paregoric–a camphorated opium-derivative–for my cracked and sore nipples. As he stood at the foot of my bed telling me about the paregoric, two nurses standing in back of him were vigorously shaking their heads no, disagreeing with what he was saying. This left me wondering whose advice I should go with. My doctor and the paregoric won.

Somehow I made it through, turning breastfeeding into a wonderful, nurturing experience *in spite of*, not *because of*, the support and rules I got in the hospital!

Tom remained my greatest supporter. I wrote him notes during the day and gave them to him when he visited in the two hours allowed for visiting each evening, inadvertently tracking the breastfeeding "wisdom" of the day. The day Melanie was born, I penned the following:

> It is now 9:00 p.m. and I'm lying here still thinking of your visit earlier this evening. Guess what? The nurse just walked in with Melanie and showed her to me and said I would start nursing tomorrow! Isn't that wonderful! Melanie opened her eyes, but had a scowl on her face, as if she resented being woken up just to visit with her mother. But soon she'll change her attitude I hope! Oh, darling, aren't we lucky and hasn't God been wonderful to us? I'm proud to have you as her father. And I know you have the essential ingredients to be a respected guide and loving protector. Today we shared a very profound experience and I love you all the more for enabling

me to share part of it with you. Tommy, the flowers smell so lovely. Did you notice that the geraniums are pink instead of the usual red? Are they pink for our little girl? Well, the nurse is about to shut the lights so I'll have to close, but remember, Tommy, I love you....

A second note ostensibly from Melanie, the next day, demonstrates that perhaps I wasn't the only one in the family who was determined to do what she knew instinctively was right:

This morning Mommy nursed me for the second time and did I play a dirty trick on her! Usually she was only supposed to nurse me five minutes the second time, but I opened my mouth really wide and held on good and tight. When she would pull me away, I would suck on my fist right away. And then she would feel sorry for me and she would cuddle me back. So I really nursed for almost a half hour. When the nurse came back, she told Mommy it was really good that I liked her so much. Did you notice how pretty I'm getting? I don't think Mother does. When I am busy thinking about something, she laughs and says "what a funny face!" so I just stop nursing and stick my lip out at her. After all I'm only 2 days, 2 hours, and 46 minutes old. Mommy said you wouldn't be able to see me till we go home. Gee, I'm going to miss your smiling face. Please don't forget your loving daughter Melanie!

Clearly, Melanie knew what *she* was doing, and was willing to be patient while I learned.

———

The little bedroom we were renting in Ken's homemade Hobby House was on the second floor. In those days new mothers weren't allowed to go up or down stairs for a couple of weeks after their delivery. But I had to get up and down to go to bed. So I did it once or twice a day (and lived to tell about it). We had cloth diapers, of course, and we kept a big pot on the stove. After washing the diapers, we'd boil them to kill all the germs.

We were supposed to have powdered formula on hand "just in case." Sterilizing procedures practically required a "hazmat" outfit. You had tongs to pick everything up with, so nothing was touched by human hands. You had to boil the bottles. You had to make the formula according to a precise regimen. It was really crazy. And then, of course, you were *not* supposed to take the baby in bed with you. So, that meant you had to sit up and nurse–I used to worry that I'd fall asleep and the baby would roll off my lap and onto the floor. That never happened, thank goodness.

The neighbors all came by to see the baby. And while I had very little work to do living in someone else's house, the care of that first baby was so overwhelming I remember saying to my mother, "Don't the neighbors realize I have a baby to take care of? I don't have time to sit and chat." With subsequent babies, on the other hand, I was practically out looking for people walking down the street to talk to and show off our new addition!

After that first baby, it's always so much easier. Experience builds confidence—and you realize that many of the things you worried about just didn't matter. Thankfully, I had my mother to rely on. I called her nearly every day, and we ate Sunday dinner with the family every week. I was incredibly lucky—my mother was a real role model for me. We talked about everything, and she was always willing to listen. Tom loved her, too. When we were engaged, I once asked Tom what he would do if we ever had a serious fight as a married couple. "I know what I'd do. I'd run right home to your mother!" was Tom's immediate reply. He and my mother had a really good relationship, and after we were married, I learned to take advantage of this. If Tom couldn't get around to fixing a broken appliance, I might bring it to my mother's house. She'd phone Tom asking for help, and he was off, lickety split, to fix it.

Within a few short months after Melanie's birth, I was pregnant with our second child. With a new baby on the way, we realized that our tiny bedroom in Ken's Hobby House could not hold two cribs and Tom and me. It was time to look for our own home. At that time, WWII veterans were given $1000 to either put towards their education or a down payment on a home. We took Tom's money and used it to buy a four room brick house in Franklin Park. There was no money left for furniture so our living room was bare for many months until relatives gave us an old living room set they were replacing. But with an empty living room or not, it was our home and we couldn't have been happier.

When I went into labor with our second baby, I didn't go into the hospital until the last minute. This was an important lesson learned from my first delivery. This time when I got to the hospital—the same hospital, the same obstetrician I'd had for Melanie's birth—my labor was so far along that I had to go right up to the delivery floor to be prepped (shaved) for delivery, while Tom stayed downstairs to sign me in. As I was getting off the elevator, I noticed a group of doctors talking a few feet away. "That Mrs. Tompson is here," one of them said. "Remember, it's 'contractions,' not 'pain.'" I immediately knew they had been reading Grantly Dick-Read's book and couldn't help but smile.

Apparently, word had spread around the hospital after my first delivery, and unbeknownst to me, a large number of physicians, residents, interns, and externs made plans to be at my next birth.

Unfortunately, my doctor had also promised his office nurse that she could attend. Because they were seeing patients at the office, Dr. O had to wait for his nurse to reschedule patients and close down the office, so he could drive her to the hospital. With the long labor for my first baby, I'm assuming he thought there was plenty of time.

Meanwhile, I was wheeled right into the delivery room and left alone. I think that none of the other doctors wanted to interfere with this unusual kind of birth. Occasionally, someone would come in and tell me to please keep my legs together or not to bear down, and then walk out. It was lonely–if only Tom could have been there to hold my hand.

Finally, my doctor arrived, and it reminded me of the triumphal procession from *Aida*. All it really lacked were the bugles. Over my shoulder, I saw the double doors burst open. First came a nurse walking backwards, putting gloves on Dr. O's outstretched hands. In back of the doctor another nurse walked, tying up his gown. Behind them marched the dozen or so spectators, who quickly encircled the delivery table.

"Doctor, they won't let me push," I said. "Marian, you can push now," he responded. Then with three pushes, no tearing, and no screaming, my beautiful dark-haired Deborah was born. As I joyfully reached out to touch her, one of the residents rushed up to my physician and said, "Doctor, how did you do it?"

Our third baby and our first red-head, Allison, was born in the hospital 20 months after Debbie's birth. I had come to realize that the only thing I didn't like about having a baby was where the birth happened. And thankfully, that was about to change.

Custom-Made Deliveries

By the time I was 25, I knew that I'd married a great guy and that I actually enjoyed being pregnant, despite the fatigue that came with mothering small children. But it would be nice to have a bit more space between my pregnancies. So after giving birth to our third child in less than three years, Tom and I decided to take the plunge and get some scientific information on fertility from our third pediatrician, Dr. J. We had tried and discarded one pediatrician with each baby. Not one of the three knew anything about breastfeeding.

So if you can imagine, here is the scenario. It was a true reflection of the times. Tom and I were sitting in the doctor's office. Dr. J had examined Allison and asked if we had any questions. "Yes," we respond, "Would you explain fertility cycles to us—how to tell when a woman is most likely to get pregnant?" Well, as a pediatrician, Dr. J obviously wasn't expecting that question! "Would you excuse me a minute," he said as he quickly walked into the other room, lit a cigarette, and then came back out to sit down directly in front of Tom. Looking straight at Tom, Dr. J explained the hows, whys, and wherefores of getting pregnant. I may as well have been in another room, as he was obviously too embarrassed to make eye contact with me.

What Dr. J left out, because he wasn't familiar with breastfeeding, was the effect of breastfeeding on ovulation. With my next baby, and yet another doctor, I learned that when exclusively breastfeeding (no bottles, no formula) and delaying the introduction of solids until the middle of the first year, our babies just naturally arrived about two years apart.

The next doctor we chose would have far-reaching effects on much more than just the spacing of our babies. Coming across Dr. Gregory White, a local doctor, was a gift beyond measure! I had read an article about Mary and Greg White and the Christian Family Movement (CFM) in the newspaper.

The Christian Family Movement at the time was a national network of families in Catholic parishes who met in each other's homes. Focused on the relationship of families to society, members sought to improve society through actions of love, service, education, and example. Even when we lived in the same town and went to the same church, I had never heard of Dr. White! That one article introduced us to a family doctor who would attend the birth of our last four children at home, and to his wife, Mary, who would become my friend and personal breastfeeding supporter, as well as a co-founder of La Leche League. We didn't have a CFM group in our parish, so Tom and I, along with some other couples and our priest, Father Hegarty, started CFM at St. John Vianny's in nearby Northlake.

Dr. Gregory and Mary White

At the time, Dr. White charged $100 for a hospital delivery and $125 if the birth took place at home. So with my fourth pregnancy, we were finally able to make plans for a home birth. This was in 1955.

At first, Tom was understandably concerned about the safety of a home birth. Although he was born at home, Tom was under the assumption held by many others in 1955 that hospital births were the epitome of safe births. Being an engineer, he had to see the facts before he could accept this "radical" idea. Luckily, a study of home births in Chicago attended by physicians from the Chicago Maternity Center had recently been published. Most of the women in the study had no or very little prenatal care. They were typically delivered on the kitchen table–for the doctor's comfort, I guess, and over a three year period, the infant mortality rate among these babies born at home was lower than in any hospital in Chicago, and not one mother had died. Tom was convinced enough to give it a try.

Home births are custom-made deliveries. During labor you are not confined to a small room or hooked up to a monitor. You can sit or walk around inside or out of the house. I felt none of the apprehension I felt in the hospital, where strange people calling me "mother" came in and poked and prodded, but would never tell me what was going on because only my doctor could do that. With a home birth, Tom and I were able to decide who would be present. I wanted Tom with me, not only for support, but just as important to share the sacred moment of birth. I was so much more relaxed, lying in my own bed, listening to Dr. White and Tom in the living room chatting about whatever interested them. "Do you think those wrestling matches on TV are faked?" I heard Tom say. As I moved toward transition and the actual delivery, the conversation stopped, and they were there only for me. Tom sat at my side reminding me to relax and take deep breaths. There is no doubt in my mind that his presence made all the difference in my birth experiences. After Laurel was born at home in our bed in 1955, Tom never saw a reason to return to a hospital birth.

One of my greatest joys during Laurel's birth was watching the wonder on Tom's face as she was born. Unlike the doctor at Deborah's birth, he understood what had happened right away. He looked at me in awe, "Marian, how did *you* do it?"

Because we were at home, I could hear his conversations as Tom phoned relatives. "Hello! Yes, Marian just had the baby! Yes, it's a girl!" I felt a little sorry for him, though, as he felt it necessary to explain that it was okay with us that we had another girl. This was our fourth daughter in a row!

And no one could take my baby away from me after the delivery to be cleaned and weighed in the nursery. Breastfeeding took place right after birth. Engorgement was never a problem. And while in those days we never considered having our other children in the room during the delivery, they were there only minutes later.

"We sat at the top of the stairs when Mom was in labor," Melanie, my first-born, recalled. "We were waiting to hear a baby cry. I used to laugh when I saw childbirth being portrayed on TV and in the movies. Never heard screaming or panic. Just heard the baby, and we were down the stairs to check out the hair color and whether or not this was another girl."

Then, after they tied a pink (or blue, later on) delivery blanket to the lamp post outside to share the good news with our neighbors, we would celebrate with a small birthday party. Sometimes the children also wrote "It's a girl!" or "It's a boy!" on pieces of paper and took them outside to let them be blown down the street by the wind!

———

Careful research comparing planned home births with hospital births continually show that without a doubt, having a baby at home is at least as safe as a hospital birth, and in most situations, home birth is safer. New sciences and new research are helping us to understand why giving birth in your own bed, surrounded by people who care for you, where you feel supported and can celebrate the birth, rather than just endure it, changes both the experience and the outcome.

When our fifth daughter, Sheila, was born in 1957, we had a reel-to-reel tape recorder which we put on the floor beside the bed. Listening to the tape, you hear newly born Sheila crying, and I'm saying, "Oh, didn't you want to leave? Didn't you want to come out? You were so comfortable in there!" I talk to her about how lovely she is. This was the only time we captured those precious moments after a birth on tape. As our life got busier and our family expanded, we just didn't remember to record a birth again. But the tape was a nice gift to give to Sheila later on as a reminder of how special her birth was.

Sheila's sisters greeting her within minutes of her birth

So now we had five girls, and like clockwork, two years later I was pregnant again. I had a strong feeling from the moment he was conceived that this baby would be a boy. And he was! Brian was born in 1959, the day before his father's birthday. What a birthday present!

The five girls wearing matching dresses made by my mom. Having them dressed alike made it easy to keep track of them when we were out in public!

When the neighbors visited after Brian's birth, they almost always said something like, "Oh, you finally got your boy!" "But we weren't trying for a boy," I tried to explain. Tom never complained that he didn't have a son. The neighbors had a different point of view. "Well, maybe Tom didn't complain, but we've noticed that with the girls he used to say, 'The baby did this, or the baby did that. When he is talking about Brian, he says, 'My *son* did this, or my *son* did that.'" So it probably was special for Tom to have a son, though without the neighbors' remarks, I might never have known.

I was really blessed that with each new pregnancy, Tom never complained. I never heard him say anything like, "Oh, no, not another child!" or "How are we going to afford it?" When a woman is pregnant, what she needs is support—and that's what he always gave me. In those days, it never occurred to us to factor in the cost of a college education as part of the cost of having a baby. Being Catholic, we just expected that we'd have babies and trusted that God would provide.

After Brian was born, I had a strong feeling that I was going to have another child, and we did. Philip was born about three and a half years after Brian— our longest space between babies. I used to tell him, "You must have been hovering around out there waiting for a chance to come into our family."

Philip was born in the fall of 1963. As I labored during the early evening, the older children waited in the living room. The bedroom window was open because it was a warm day, and I remember hearing the crinkle-crinkle-crinkle sound of someone walking on the dry leaves. It was six-year-old Sheila, peering in the open window. She couldn't see in the window because the shade was drawn. But she could hear Tom and me talking, and when the baby was born, she wanted to be the first one to know if it was a boy or a girl. We could tell she was there, but we didn't shoo her away. It must have made a good impression because later Sheila's daughters, Sarah and Rebekah, were also born at home. Sarah's birth was attended by Dr. White in the same room and the same bed where Sheila had been born.

———

In those days, getting married usually meant the wife would quit her job, if she had one, to stay home and raise a family. Obviously, I thrived in that environment. We ended up five short of my original goal of a dozen children, but by then, living with the reality of a large family, it was okay. Seven seemed like a good number, the perfect number for Tom and me.

As our young family grew, so did my gratitude for my other important source of support: my mother. When a new baby arrived, my mother was always there to help with the cooking or cleaning or whatever needed to be done. She said to me more than once, "Marian, when you are older, it's important to feel that you are needed." As a young mother who loved her children dearly, but found herself with many new decisions to make, my mother was a great sounding board.

I would phone her every morning at 8:00 am after she had gotten my brother off to school, and she would greet me as if this were the bright spot of her day. She rarely gave unsolicited advice or found fault with what I was doing. She would empathize with what I was experiencing ("Oh I remember being so tired, too!") and rarely checked to see if I had followed any suggestions she might have made. Mostly, she just listened and helped me to enjoy my children by understanding what I was going through and supporting me in following my instincts—even if, like breastfeeding and home birth, they were contrary to popular practices of the time.

Things were happening that I couldn't know at the time would be moving me along on a journey I never would have imagined. I was learning to trust my instincts. I had the loving support of Tom and my mother, and I was blessed with the great good fortune of meeting so many other people, who, as they came into my life, also brought me the inspiration and practical advice I needed. They were all paving the way for another phase of my passionate journey.

Doing the Right Thing After All

During the past 50 years, I can't tell you how often a mother or father has come up to me at an LLL gathering and admitted that as a result of being in La Leche League, they were parenting their children so differently than they had originally expected to and so differently from the way they had been brought up. "I'll kill myself if they don't turn out" was a common refrain.

We all want to do the best for our children. So what led me to make the kind of choices I did? First of all, I was influenced by the way I was raised and by the aunts and uncles who surrounded me. Then there were books that impressed me: *Childbirth Without Fear* and *Cheaper by the Dozen*. Though I didn't realize it at the time, I think being fully "present" during a planned, unmedicated birth also had an influence. Birth is a holy moment, and I've even seen a father drastically change his expectation of the kind of parenting his newborn needed, just because he was present when his daughter was born. This particular man's mother had worked throughout his childhood, and he just expected his wife would do the same. But being present at the birth of his first born buried that notion in his mind forever.

A commitment to breastfeeding has another huge influence. All that skin-to-skin contact and closeness evokes a hormonal response that creates a different kind of bond between a mother and her baby. I remember telling Tom after Melanie was born that even if breastfeeding was no better than formula-feeding, I wanted to breastfeed all my babies because that closeness felt so good. It was the effect of my choices, along with the people those choices brought into my life, that supported and shaped my parenting.

With our first three daughters born in less than three years, it seemed like I was always holding a baby or toddler, or both. Tom would leave in the morning while I sat in the rocking chair in the living room nursing the baby, with Melanie and Deborah playing on the floor beside me. As often as not, he would come home at the end of the day and walk in the door to see me rocking the baby, with the toddlers still close at hand. When the baby cried, I would pick her up. Much of my housework didn't get done because the children came first, and I began to wonder if something was wrong with me. My neighbors, most of whom were bottle-feeding and living by the four-hour feeding schedule, seemed to be so much better organized. Their houses always looked neat and tidy. I secretly suspected it was a weakness in me that led me to carry my baby around because I couldn't stand to let her cry. It took a while, but I finally came to believe that it was probably the effect of my birth and breastfeeding experiences that helped mold me into the kind of mother my babies needed.

Snuggling baby Brian

Few women breastfed at that time, and many were not even aware that it was an option. One day at the grocery store, Philip, who was only a few weeks old and lying in the cart, started to cry as one of my neighbors came down the aisle. "Oh, time for a bottle!" she said as she passed by. "Oh, no, he's never had a bottle," was my response. My neighbor skidded to a stop, turning her cart around to get back to me again. "You mean he's drinking from a cup already?" she asked incredulously. That Philip might be breastfed never entered her mind.

Babies were not usually taken out to public gatherings in those days, especially in the evening. It was expected they would be left at home with a baby sitter and a bottle. Many times our baby was the only infant present when we attended talks about the family. The few baby carriers available in those days were usually slings designed to help support an older baby on his mother's hip. But then I read a magazine article about a couple who wore their baby in a carrier on their back when hiking in the mountains. This was before carriers with metal frames were invented, so a baby had to be at least six months old before it could be used. But it seemed like such a great way to carry the baby, while having your hands free to hold on to other children. I wrote to the magazine, got in touch with the couple in the article, and discovered the Gerry Carrier, and voila! Mary White and I soon sent off for our own. We never did use them in the mountains, as Franklin Park is pretty flat, but they sure made it easier to take baby along, no matter what we were doing.

For the first three months of his life, Phillip needed to be
close to me, and stayed cozy in the Mexican rebozo

Around this time, Mary told me about a lecture series on parenting being given by Dr. Herbert Ratner, the Health Commissioner of the city of

Oak Park. The first one Tom and I attended covered the "terrible twos" and the "trusting threes." Typically, the evening started with a film from Canada showing children of that age in real life situations. Then Dr. Ratner opened up the discussion to the parents. Everyone was welcome to ask questions. Dr. Ratner spoke about that particular developmental stage and gave suggestions on how to handle different kinds of situations that might arise. It was a perspective that resonated deeply with my own mothering style. Walking out of the auditorium, it was with a great sense of relief that I turned to Tom and said, "We have been doing the right thing after all!" How liberating it was to have Dr. Ratner's validation! From then on, I could keep on picking up my babies, enjoy the toddlers, and ignore the dust bunnies under the couch and not feel guilty about it.

Dr. Ratner also said something else that evening that further endeared him to me: "Show me a mother with a perfectly clean house and I'll show you a woman with serious psychological problems." Little did we know then that Dr. Ratner was not only to become an important person in our family's life, but that his philosophy would later permeate the lives of thousands, probably millions, of families through La Leche League.

I once again began to find myself out of step with the modern woman when Betty Friedan's book, *The Feminine Mystique,* came out. In 1964 she was the keynote speaker at a meeting of the Maternal and Child Health Association in Springfield, Illinois. Dr. Ratner drove several of us to the meeting. This included three-and-a-half month old Philip and Melanie who would celebrate her 14th birthday that weekend. During the keynote, Philip wanted to nurse, so I opted to go into the bathroom and stood there nursing him when a young nurse burst through the door. "Isn't it wonderful what Betty Freidan says," she exclaimed, "how we can measure our worth, just by getting a job!" But then she paused, noticing Philip nursing, and said, "But I'm so glad my mother didn't feel that way."

Why was I in the bathroom nursing? Well, I had been sitting at a round table with six or seven doctors and was quite certain they would be very uncomfortable if I started nursing Philip in front of them. That would make me uncomfortable, too, and I just didn't want to have to deal with it.

The next day at a breakout session, Betty Friedan went into more detail about why it was important for a woman to have a paycheck as a confirmation of her worth. So I stood up, Philip in my arms, and explained that just seeing Philip breastfeeding, happy, and healthy, and knowing how I contributed to this was all the justification I needed to feel important as a woman. With that, Ms. Friedan walked over to me, drew herself up, and said, "You are building up your self esteem at the expense of your baby!" Imagine! I realized then that we were the product of two very different life experiences, and she might never understand why I enjoyed and valued being a mother.

So by 1956, I was the happy, though often tired, mother of four beautiful daughters under the age of seven, I was married to an incredibly supportive husband, and I'd met five people who would become key players in the rest of my life: Doctors Ratner and White, Mary White, Edwina Froehlich, and Betty Wagner, who, along with three other women I was soon to meet, would become the cornerstone of an effort that would ultimately affect mothers and babies around the world.

A walk in the park with my parents and children

When You See a Problem

8

Little did I know when Tom and I set off with our four children to attend a Christian Family Movement picnic at Wilder Park in Elmhurst, Illinois, in the summer of 1956, that it would be another one of those pivotal moments in my life. It was a beautiful, sunny day, and I was delighted to see Mary and Greg White there with their six children. The White's were CFM members in St. Gertrude's Church in Franklin Park, and Tom and I belonged to the CFM group at St. John Vianny's Church in nearby Northlake.

As Mary and I sat together under a shade tree talking and nursing and watching the older children play, women we knew came by and started talking about breastfeeding. It turned out that they had wanted to nurse their babies, too. But faced with many of the same situations we had encountered, along with a lack of support from their doctors, they ended up formula-feeding their babies. This was an epiphany for me! Until that day, I was unaware that other women had faced the same roadblocks to breastfeeding as Mary and I had. Even Mary had some difficulties with breastfeeding, despite being married to a supportive husband. She, too, had to learn what did and didn't work by trial and error. Women didn't talk to each other about such intimate things in those days, and it was startling to learn that several of our friends were bottle-feeding their babies *as their second choice.*

It must have been seeing Mary and me with our nursing babies that triggered the conversations, and it began to bother me that women who wanted to do the very best for their babies couldn't get the information and support they needed in order to breastfeed.

But maybe there was *something* we could do. The Christian Family Movement encouraged social action: "When you see a problem, what do you do about it?" Tom and I had moved out of Franklin Park by that time, and after the picnic, I'd stop by Mary's house when I was in town to talk about what we might do. There was very little written about breastfeeding in those days. The only book Mary found was written by a male physician who, while well-intentioned, had some strange suggestions. For example, if the baby wasn't taking in enough milk, he recommended the mother give the baby an enema before a feeding! We finally decided that the most helpful thing to do would be to bring together women who had breastfed to share their experiences and practical advice with mothers seeking help. Mother-to-mother support was not a new idea—women have been supporting other women for millennia, but this would be an organized effort to take advantage of the natural way women have of helping each other.

The Whites and Tompsons on an outing

I called Edwina Froehlich and asked if she would participate. Edwina and her husband, John, also belonged to St. Gertrude's CFM. Edwina was in her 30's when she married and now had two boys, and although the Froehlich's hadn't attended the picnic, Edwina was the only person in town besides Mary and myself that I knew had breastfed. That's how little women talked about breastfeeding in those days. Because babies weren't nursed in public and even formula-fed babies were usually left at home with a sitter, how a baby was being fed was rarely part of a conversation.

Edwina immediately agreed to help out and invited Viola Lennon, another breastfeeding mother she knew from their work in the Young Christian Workers.

Mary White invited her sister-in-law, Mary Ann Kerwin, who was nursing her first baby, as well as Mary White's friend, Mary Ann Cahill, who was also in CFM. I had never met these two women before. Mary Ann Cahill invited Betty Wagner who had been very helpful when Mary Ann Cahill was breastfeeding. I had met Betty briefly in 1952, when she was an election judge and I voted in my first presidential election.

We were just "typical" 1950s moms—some had more money than others; some had more children than others. We didn't have that polished look of mothers so popular on early television shows, dressed in heels, a skirt and twin sweater set, looking like we were going out to work, rather than staying at home. On second thought, I have to admit that Viola, on her way to becoming the mother of ten children, usually did fit that polished look.

The seven of us got together at Mary White's house to organize. And organize we did! I suggested that Edwina be the president. She was the oldest. She already had experience as president of the Young Christian Workers and had even been to Europe in that role. I thought she would be perfect for the job. So after making what seemed like the obvious nomination, I went to the kitchen for a moment, and when I came back out, Mary said, "Marian, this was *your* idea, so you have to be president!" I was too shy to make a fuss about it and agreed. After all, in a small town like Franklin Park, how much work could being president be?

Six of the Founders got together at Edwina's house

We decided on what should be covered in a series of five monthly meetings, and then held our first meeting in October of 1956 at the White's house in Franklin Park. We invited the women we knew from church and a few patients of Dr. White came at his suggestion.

Each meeting had a theme and the general plan was to introduce the theme, talk about it, and then open the meeting for discussion. We sat in a circle to facilitate this. Because there was so little in print at the time that validated breastfeeding, I read an article recently published in *Reader's Digest* entitled, "Breast Fed is Best Fed," at the first meeting. This was a great entrée into the theme for that evening, "The Advantages of Breastfeeding." The women then shared their stories and asked their questions, and looked forward to coming back the following month.

As important as mother-to-mother support was, we were aware that husbands, as the first line of support, also needed more information about breastfeeding. Most women in those days would be too embarrassed to discuss breastfeeding in front of other men. So from the beginning, we had a separate fifth meeting for fathers led by Dr. Ratner and Dr. White. Checking out a doctor's house was always a draw, and the beer that was available probably made it even more enjoyable. Women weren't allowed! Men, just like women, sometimes had questions that might embarrass their spouses, and we wanted the men to feel comfortable enough to talk about anything on their minds. From the little bit that Tom told me, I learned that the men left the meeting empowered and with a different appreciation of their role as dads and babies in general. The doctors helped the men see they weren't just substitute mothers. They weren't just "filling in" for their wives. Other babies cried. Other babies woke up at night, and other couples were exhausted. Fathers had a unique and important role, both in supporting their wives and in their relationship with the baby.

With monthly meetings for the women and quarterly meetings for the men, we seemed to have a doable plan in place. And it shouldn't take too much time out of our lives. With breastfeeding of newborns in the hospital in 1956 estimated at 18 to 20% in the United States, how many of those mothers would be living in Franklin Park? In a few years, we should be finished with this project and be able to move on to other things.

As the newly appointed president of this effort to help breastfeeding mothers in our community, I was already looking forward to my retirement.

Women Taking Charge

Wait—did I say *retirement? Soon?* It's true that I was pregnant again with my fifth child when I was elected president. And there are people who believe that women lose some of their brain cells with each pregnancy, but I don't think any of the seven of us were looking much beyond helping women we knew or those Dr. White sent to our meetings. Busy with our own growing families, we hardly had time to think further ahead than what had to be done on the day in front of us.

At the same time, Tom and I were also taking children from a nearby orphanage for weekends at our house. This was part of a church project to acquaint children living in institutions with family life. We became very fond of Nancy, Bobby, and Terry, siblings whose mother was not in a position to care for them. This led Tom and I to become foster parents when Nancy graduated from eighth grade and had to find a temporary home outside the orphanage.

Being foster parents eventually led to a number of children being placed with us for a few days or a weekend while arrangements were made to get them out of unsafe situations. Our children took this all in stride and, in fact, seemed to enjoy having unexpected visitors.

What we hadn't counted on with helping breastfeeding mothers was that word of the meetings would so quickly spread and that women from nearby towns, and even as far away as Chicago, were soon showing up at Mary's door. It was becoming clear that our initial assumption of how many mothers were interested in breastfeeding was a bit low. Each meeting was a surprise as growing numbers of women filled the White's living room. Before our first series of meetings was finished, it was apparent that there had to be two meetings a month if we were to handle the crowd, and Edwina quickly volunteered to host a second group at her house.

While we were teaching the women about breastfeeding, we were learning a lot from them as well. Most mothers, for example, were drugged during their delivery, meaning they didn't get to breastfeed the baby for hours or longer after birth. Even after my unmedicated births in the hospital, I wasn't allowed to breastfeed until the next day. In the meantime, babies were given bottles, which interfered with getting breastfeeding off to a good start. So we decided to include a discussion of childbirth in the meetings and the effect it had on the initiation of breastfeeding.

Once mothers started out giving the best to their babies with breastfeeding, they wanted to continue with good nutrition, as they started solids around the middle of the first year. So a discussion on nutrition was added. We all began reading labels and baking our own bread. The amount of emphasis on nutrition at a meeting depended on who was leading the meeting. Edwina, without a doubt, was the shining star here. We started making our own granola and yogurt. I loved my recipe for granola so much I couldn't wait to get up in the morning to have breakfast!

And we soon had a name. In the 50s, not only was *seeing* a breastfeeding woman in public rare, but even *saying* "breast" in polite company or putting it in print in a meeting notice was unheard of. Dr. White came to our rescue. He suggested naming our fledgling organization for a shrine to the Spanish Madonna, located in St. Augustine, Florida, *Nuestra Senora de La Leche y Buen Parto*–Our Lady of Plentiful Milk and Happy Delivery. "La Leche" was the perfect secret code word, and so we became "La Leche League." We liked the name and what it stood for, but as the League grew, it was one that we would be pronouncing and explaining for years to come.

In 1957 we heard that Dr. Grantly Dick-Read, the author of *Childbirth Without Fear*, was coming to the United States and stopping in Chicago to speak to physicians. As women who had unmedicated births because of his book, we were very eager to meet him, so Edwina wrote asking if he could come to Franklin Park. We were disappointed when he replied that he would rather give a talk to the public than just meet with us, and assured us that if we could set something up, his name would draw enough people to cover his $700 fee. $700? How could we possibly raise $700? As it turned out–as things often happened in LLL in those early days, we raised more than the $700–Dr. Dick-Read was right!

Edwina, baby Peter, and I talk with Dr. Dick-Read

But first we had to get the word out. Because we had no mailing lists to use, we printed fliers and sent them to everyone we thought would be remotely interested. Only one Chicago newspaper would print a small notice–and that was after checking with the American Medical Association. To our amazement, we ended up filling the 1250-seat Franklin Park High School auditorium with people who came from three states. We turned away hundreds more!

It was a sign of the times and the role of women in the 1950s that compelled the husband of one of the founders to take me aside to explain that while I was probably planning on introducing Dr. Dick-Read myself, the doctor was such a important person it would be much more appropriate that he be introduced by a man! I thanked him for his suggestion, but as a woman who had had five natural childbirths at the time as a result of Dr. Dick-Read's teachings, I thought I was more than qualified to introduce him myself.

As part of his talk, Dr. Dick-Read showed a film of three unmedicated births. It was very unusual in those days to see a movie about birth, and these were the first "natural" births that most of the audience had seen. Even so, I was mystified at the remark of a local doctor as he exited the auditorium grumbling to his companion that "those births had to be fake." Was he so out of touch that he didn't recognize childbirth as Nature intended?

We had been wanting to print information sheets for mothers who contacted us by mail, and now after paying Dr. Dick-Read's fee, we had money left over to do so. Responding to individual letters from mothers was a labor of love that also produced some guilt in me. Because time was of the essence in responding to mothers with a question or a problem, this meant I was then ignoring writing to relatives because there just wasn't enough time in my life. Staying in touch with relatives by phone was too expensive in those days, and email wouldn't appear on the scene for decades!

Those letters not only confirmed the value of mother-to-mother help, but they were also an unmatched source of information on the challenges breastfeeding mothers encountered. There was also a similarity to many of the problems, so we decided to put together a printed course by mail which could be sent out to interested mothers and which we naively hoped would help to save time with our written responses.

That Course by Mail became the first *Womanly Art of Breastfeeding*. It was an early pre-computer version of self-publishing. We printed it and held it together in a little three-clip colored folder. At first, we were going to send out a chapter at a time, but it quickly became apparent that it was more sensible to put all 31 pages together and sell it for $2.00. A personal letter accompanied each copy inviting the mother to write back if she had questions that still needed answering.

At the same time I decided to start a newsletter as a way of keeping isolated mothers in touch with other breastfeeding mothers. If they didn't have an LLL group to attend, where were women going to hear those inspiring and practical stories from other breastfeeding mothers?

So I would sit at the dining room table with a portable typewriter typing out the *LLL News* on those horrible purple gelatin sheets needed for mimeographing. We sent out 100 copies of the first issue free, asking people if they would like to subscribe at $1.00 a year for six issues. Mary White came over to help with the stapling and folding of that first issue, and my seven-year-old daughter, Deb, was captured to lick the stamps.

During the next five years, we sold 17,000 copies of the first edition of the *Womanly Art*. It hadn't been out long before we realized that we had to write another book incorporating all that we were learning from the breastfeeding mothers who had become part of our lives. So we started getting together to write the next edition. Doctors Ratner and White again checked our information for medical accuracy. Mary Carson, an experienced editor, provided us with an organizational structure for the book and did the index. An artist and breastfeeding mother, Joy Sidor, grateful for the help she received with breastfeeding her baby, provided winsome line drawings that gave a new attractive look to nursing mothers. Five years and ten babies later, we had a completed manuscript. And in 1963, the blue-covered *Womanly Art of Breastfeeding* made its debut.

This second edition was also self-published. This time we used a printer from downstate Illinois who had been recommended by Mary Carson. We got a little nervous when we learned that in order to get the best price break we would have to print 10,000 copies! But the printer agreed to let us make monthly payments instead of paying up front all at once. It turned out to be one of the best business decisions he ever made.

In May, 1963, the very same month our new *Womanly Art* made its debut, *Reader's Digest* came out with an excerpt from Karen Pryor's book, *Nursing Your Baby*. It was a chapter entitled, "They Teach the Joys of Breastfeeding," and it was all about La Leche League! Within a few months, all 10,000 books had been sold, and we were on to our next printing.

Obviously, there was a change in the air. Mothers were ready to take charge of their lives. And when it came to breastfeeding, the seven of us found ourselves leading the way!

10

Lipstick, Confession, and "That Crazy Woman"

⟡

While the seven of us worked as a team, making use of each others' strengths, I became the spokeswoman for LLL by virtue of my role as president. How ironic–shy Marian Leonard Tompson was now *president* of an organization that was quickly growing well beyond Franklin Park. As interest in breastfeeding spread, so did requests to speak, first on local radio and TV stations, and then on panels before medical groups, and ultimately at symposiums and conferences around the world.

Having the involvement of Doctors White and Ratner from the beginning to check our material for accuracy gave La Leche League a credibility we would not have had otherwise. The doctors also gave us a foot in the door with the medical community. In 1961, Dr. Ratner invited me to participate on a panel at a meeting of the Illinois State Medical Society. Although I had the comfort of knowing that Dr. White would be there as another panelist, I was nervous. So I did what needed to be done: I went to the store and bought a tube of courage–a red lipstick named encouragingly, "Bold"! The shade wasn't important. It was perception that I needed.

Dr. Herbert Ratner

But boldness couldn't cover my naivety. While I was sitting in the hallway with another speaker, Dr. Robert Jackson, the doctor struck up a conversation and asked me where I had gone to school. Happy to have someone to talk with, I quickly gave him the name of my grammar school and my three high schools. It wasn't until years later that I realized all he wanted to know was where I had gone to college–I was clueless and degreeless! And Dr. Jackson was too much of a gentleman to let me know.

The next year I was asked to speak on breastfeeding at the International Childbirth Education Association conference in Seattle, Washington. This meant taking my first commercial airplane ride. While I had a short flight in a Piper Cub with Tom years before, the trip to Seattle was serious flying, farther away from home than I'd ever been.

Figuring I'd need all the help I could get, especially if the plane was going to crash with me on board, I asked the priest at our church if I could go to confession before I left town. If the plane crashed and I was about to die, I couldn't be too careful. Ordinarily confessions were heard on Saturday, but Father said he would make an exception and hear my confession on Sunday during mass, right before I left town.

The following Sunday, with the church filled with people, the priest came out and walked into the confessional. And then I went into the side of the confessional, where penitents knelt. Parishioners must have thought I had committed murder or done something equally unspeakable that I was so desperate to confess during Mass. Come to think of it, Father was probably scratching his head, too, when I confessed to simple things like forgetting my prayers or getting angry. I couldn't worry about what went through anyone else's mind, but I declared my sins and was forgiven.

Later that day, Tom drove me to the airport, chatting away in what was probably an attempt to distract me from my nervousness. But all I could think was, "How can he be so relaxed when we might not ever *see* each other again?!"

I boarded the plane and sat down. I was in the middle seat and kept trying to look out the window. Finally, when the man sitting next to the window learned it was my first plane ride, he switched seats with me. I guess he didn't want me leaning over him the entire flight. My face was glued to the window all the way across the country.

This was an airplane with propellers, and they didn't go as high as the jet planes do now, so I had a great view of the country. At one point I noticed what looked like flames coming out of one of the propellers! When I called the stewardess to alert her of this impending disaster, she said, "Oh, no, that's just normal." It seemed that I was going to survive the flight after all.

We had to land first in Portland, Oregon, before taking off again for Seattle. And since Seattle was so close, the plane didn't go up as high, and once again I was sure we would crash–so far from home! If I was going to die, I wanted it to happen closer to home. Eventually, we landed safely in Seattle, and I quickly realized how much better it was to travel by plane because it didn't keep me away from home as long as other kinds of transportation would. Given how much flying I would be doing in the years to come, this timesaver would become even more important to me.

I gave my speech, followed by one from a doctor who really didn't know much of anything about breastfeeding. He *thought* he did, but he was really quite uninformed. Even the audience realized it. People later told me they were surprised I didn't attack him, or get angry at him, or try to show him up. What would have been the point? As a student, he had probably been taught little, if anything, about breastfeeding in medical school. And given the low rates of breastfeeding at the time, it was unlikely he had many breastfeeding mothers to learn from. I felt it would be unfair to attack this man because of his particular life journey. He just wasn't aware of how much he didn't know until he agreed to speak at the conference.

Walking back to my seat, I overheard someone say, "Someday Grandma Tompson is going to be on the moon, teaching people how to breastfeed."

Fortunately, that prophecy has not come true —yet! While Tom would have loved to meet such a challenge, I prefer to have my feet planted firmly on earth.

I was always a little nervous before any public appearance. What really fed into my nervousness, especially during the time I was president, was not letting down LLL Leaders, or disappointing them in the way LLLI was represented. For many Leaders, a television show would be the first and maybe only time they saw a La Leche League founder, and I wanted them to be proud of our organization and what we stood for.

Dr. Ratner was responsible for introducing LLL to the Illinois Maternal and Child Health Association. For years he drove several of us downstate to their annual conference, where we had opportunities to listen to talks and meet a lot of doctors. Although LLL had no money to rent exhibit space, Dr. Ratner would somehow find a card table and set it up in the exhibit hall alongside all the commercial exhibits, so we could display LLL material we brought with us. It's a tribute to Dr. Ratner that we got away with it!

One year, I was invited to participate in a panel discussion on childbirth at the Maternal and Child Health meeting. The event, billed as a Town Hall Meeting, was to be open to the public for the first time. I was told there would be several doctors and an OB nurse on the panel, and I was asked to present a mother's point of view. Well, that sounded easy enough, four of us sitting around a table and talking about childbirth. But when the evening arrived and I walked on stage, there was no table, only chairs in a straight line facing the audience. When the first doctor, an obstetrician, was introduced, he got up, walked to a microphone with some papers in his hand, and *read* a speech about the benefits of obstetrical care. Next, the pediatrician was introduced, and he got up and also read a speech on the breakthroughs in pediatrics. The obstetrical nurse had her speech written and ready. No one had mentioned anything to me about writing a speech for our panel discussion. And now it was my turn! So I walked to the front of the stage with my hands at my side and I simply talked about the natural births of the six children I had at the time. I shared that because I was awake for my first three deliveries in the hospital, I knew firsthand how poorly suited hospitals were to meet the needs of laboring women. Because my hospital deliveries had been more of a hindrance than a help, I had opted to have my last three children at home. I wasn't angry or judgmental; I simply told my story.

The effect was explosive. Doctors jumped up from the audience to contest what I had said. One physician, shouting from the back of the room, accused me of making my story up and said that if he could put it in a book he would make thousands of dollars. After I left the stage, I was accosted by a doctor's wife who backed me into a corner and accused me of damaging her poor husband's reputation. It even made headlines in the local newspaper the next day: a full page spread with photos and a story on how a mother put the professionals in their place.

The following year, at the next meeting of the Association, Dr. Ratner invited me to lunch with some other doctors. As we sat and chatted, one of the doctors said, "Do you remember that crazy woman who talked about her births last year?" And Dr. Ratner said, "You're sitting right next to her." Oh, the look on that poor doctor's face. It was priceless. And, what was really ironic? All I did was talk about wanting an unmedicated birth and share the fact that with my first three children I learned that the hospitals weren't set up for it. That, and to share the experience with Tom, was the reason I had the rest of my babies at home.

I wasn't trying to start a revolution with the speeches I gave and the choices I made–I simply wanted to be true to myself and provide what I knew in my heart was best for me and my babies. I wasn't aware of how many other women, who until now had not had a voice, wanted the same things and were willing to break down every last barrier that stood in their way. And there I was, behind my "Bold" lipstick, tearing away at those walls.

11

Breastfeeding Goes to Capitol Hill

~✑~

As LLL continued to grow, my involvement in it and the time it took me away from my family grew as well. Even today, I always seem to be going from one deadline to the next, but luckily during the early days those deadlines were far apart.

It had originally been my dream that once our first LLL convention in 1964 and the International Childbirth Education Association Convention that followed it were over, our family would drive to the Outer Banks off the coast of North Carolina and just sit and relax by the water. I had read about the islands, and they seemed like what we could use after the busyness of the conventions. I could just picture Tom and me in beach chairs or walking along the water with the children. I could almost smell the salt air! But it was just a dream; we never actually got there. It was just as well, because my life, as it turned out, had other plans.

Instead, as soon as I got home from the two conventions, Dr. White asked me to take care of a four-month-old exclusively breastfed baby for a week while her mother was hospitalized. All of a sudden I was nursing two babies and building up an incredible supply of milk to take care of our breastfeeding visitor, as well as my eight-month-old son. So, in a way, I did get a chance to sit around a lot while nursing the two babies. It never occurred to me that it wouldn't work or that I wouldn't have enough milk. I had such respect for Dr. White that if he thought it would work, I expected it would. And it did. The visiting baby seemed quite happy in our house. And with six other children to play with, it all seemed to work out. Either that or I've blanked it out of my mind—I'm not quite sure. The only problem was that after she left my breasts were bursting with milk.

At the same time, I was always keeping my eye out for someone else who might be willing to be president. In those days, we felt that the president had to live in or near Franklin Park and have a husband who was willing to go along with her added responsibilities. I never found that person, and one summer I felt quite strongly the need to take some time off. My family had not complained about my busyness, but I just felt that I wasn't giving them enough of the individual attention they each deserved. So I asked the other founders if I could take a leave of absence. And they agreed. We were leaving that weekend to drive to a farm near the Mississippi River owned by some friends. It was a warm, sunny day, so the windows in the car were open. I can still feel the air on my face and the exhilaration I felt at being set free. We had a lovely couple of days at the farm, but when I got home, there was no one available to do my LLL work, and almost as quickly as it started, my leave of absence was over, and I was back to being president.

The second La Leche League convention was held in Indiana in 1966. In order to get there, the founders had to cover their own transportation expenses, which was no small feat in our family. The cheapest way I could get there was by bus, but, at the time, we didn't even have enough money for that.

Reluctantly, I took a job waitressing for a local caterer in the evening. I hated it. First of all, I was already tired at the end of a full day of caring for my family and doing LLL work. And the events were poorly organized. I remember one evening when the food wasn't ready on time and anger among the diners was growing. As we finally started walking out with food to our assigned tables, people sitting at other tables just grabbed the plates out of our hands. They were hungry and mad at having to wait so long to eat. I couldn't blame them for being angry—or hungry. As soon as I had earned enough money to cover my bus fare, I quit.

Once we realized that conferences were going to be a fact of our LLLI life, cost of transportation for the founders was factored into the conference budget. We were expected to be at the conferences. We wanted to be there to meet the Leaders who were representing LLL all over the world, and never again did I have to work for that caterer in order to pay my way.

As the number of Leaders grew, so did the number of doctors who joined us. I met a pediatrician, Dr. Robert Mendelsohn, at an Illinois Maternal and Child Health meeting in 1962. Dr. Mendelsohn gave a talk about the importance of parents staying with their hospitalized children—a radical idea at the time. Equally radical was his assertion that patients could *question* the kind of medical care their child was receiving. This was back in the day when parents were just considered visitors to their sick children in the hospital and, therefore, subject to the posted visiting hours. It was a time when the word of a doctor was accepted without question. Dr. Mendelsohn's views were startling to hear from a medical professional–but so reassuring. I knew how important his talk would be to other mothers, so I introduced myself to him and got his permission to make his talk available as an LLL handout. He would soon join the newly-formed LLLI Medical Advisory Board. He became another lifelong friend.

In 1969 the husband of an LLL member who worked for the government arranged for me and several doctors on our Medical Advisory Board to be invited to the White House Conference on Food, Nutrition, and Health to be held that December in Washington, DC.

Drs. Robert Mendelsohn and Derrick Jelliffe at the WHite House conference

I had a reservation at the hotel for a single room, but when I got there, late at night, the single rooms were all gone, and the hotel offered to put three late arrivals in the "Presidential Suite," charging each of us the same price as a single room. During the day, LLL Leaders in the DC area were able to enjoy this massive suite that included a grand piano in the living room. My bedroom was huge–it had two closets, one for each of the dresses I had brought with me.

On the floor above was the suite where Vice President Agnew and his wife were staying while their house was being repaired. One evening, getting on the elevator outside the suite, I found it occupied by the vice president's wife and two Secret Service agents. As soon as we said, "Hello," an agent immediately pressed the button, and we went straight down to the garage without a stop. It took me awhile to realize that the only reason the agents let the elevator stop for me was their assumption that someone in the Presidential Suite was safe to let on the elevator with the Vice President's wife!

This White House Conference in 1969 represented a new and different kind of role for LLL and for me, and I must admit feeling a bit uncomfortable in it. Instead of just making ourselves available to mothers who wanted our help, it was our job to persuade doctors, nurses, nutritionists, and other health educators of the importance of breastfeeding, so they would encourage and support it. There was more than a little irony in all this that the responsibility of convincing the medical profession of the value of breastfeeding fell to mothers, whose personal experiences were so convincing they didn't need the scientific backing to validate breastfeeding. And there was already a growing body of scientific evidence–of which far too many healthcare professionals were seemingly unaware.

It wasn't easy, even in our workshop on the pregnant and nursing mother. I had seen firsthand how emotional women could be when discussing this topic–mothers who had wanted to breastfeed, but didn't get the information and support they needed and felt the loss years later–but its effect on the men was no less explosive. We tried to read a statement proposing the promotion and encouragement of breastfeeding by governmental agencies and offered the cooperation of the League in any appropriate manner. Objections were raised to all but the most general of statements on breastfeeding to be included in the recommendations to President Nixon.

"It's never been proven that breastfeeding is best." "Why, then we'll be coming out *against* bottle-feeding!" "You can never reverse a trend after it's started, and breastfeeding is losing popularity." "The labor unions and industry will be mad at us because breastfeeding women can't work." This is what some of the other participants had to say.

Where was the support for something we found so obvious among the attendees at our workshop, which included many nationally prominent doctors? Add to this, the bias of the facilitator, a pediatrician, who made objective discussion virtually impossible. "If you're going to mention advantages of breastfeeding, be sure and list the disadvantages, also," he insisted.

The LLL dad who worked for the government suggested we hold a press conference. A press conference! Wow, we had never done a press conference before. LLL Leaders made up signs that said, "Prevent malnutrition in our American babies, Public briefing 5 pm, President's Conference 'ignores' most economical way to promote healthy children" and taped them up on the walls around the hotel. We had no idea if anyone would come.

But people did come, packing the room. There were reporters from at least seven newspapers, government officials, conference participants, and, of course, League mothers and Leaders, with their beautiful babies and toddlers in tow. We made new contacts and friends who would help us in the years to come, and it became increasingly apparent that where the optimal good health of our children is concerned, breastfeeding had become an issue that couldn't be ignored.

The next day, when some of us were leaving for the airport, a reporter from Minneapolis, who had been at our press conference, asked if he could share our cab. Several days later, I was sent a clipping from a Minneapolis newspaper written by that very reporter. He described the conference and our press conference, and he wrote that while LLL was talking about the importance of saving money by breastfeeding, they were staying in the "Presidential Suite" of the Park Sheraton Hotel! And to think we made room for him on our ride to the airport! If he had only asked us why we were in the Presidential Suite, he would have known that it was a bargain!

I made a lot of trips through the years and went to a lot of fascinating places, but, as saintly as it sounds, my number one priority was always my family. I just didn't like leaving them. Traveling wouldn't have been possible without a husband who remembered what it was like when we had nowhere to turn for breastfeeding support, and without a mother who lived nearby and felt it was important to be "needed."

My family kept my feet on the ground and kept me in check with the real world. I'll always remember flying home from a trip to California. The California Leaders gave me a bouquet of flowers as I was leaving and accompanied me to the gate at the airport. When I walked outside to board the plane, there was a red carpet leading up the stairs. Then I got off the plane at O'Hare where I was met at the gate by Tom and the children. They crowded around me, all talking at once. "Mommy, I need this for school tomorrow!" "I have to have this ironed!" I had to chuckle at the comparison of walking up the red carpet, flowers in my arms while getting on the plane in California, and then getting off at O'Hare. I was right back to a chorus of little voices–and loving it.

Difficult as it may be to believe, Tom never complained about problems that came up when I was gone or because I was gone. We had a world map on the dining room wall with stars pasted on the places I had traveled, and there were always homemade "welcome home" signs and decorations put up by the children for my return. The children knew that if they had a problem with me leaving, then I would stay home, but the one time this happened was far off in my future when my daughter Melanie was expecting her first baby the same week I was to be in Austria, as the first lay person invited to address the Austrian Pediatric Society. Because my name was on the program, I still had to write my talk that was then translated and given by LLL Leader Eleanor Randall, accompanied by Edwina Froehlich. I'm so glad I stayed home and welcomed not one baby, but two, as Melanie gave birth to twin boys, Nate and Ben!

Long distance phone calls were very expensive in those days, so I would make only one call home to let the family know I arrived safely. I soon realized the house could be falling down behind him, but Tom's invariable reassurance that "everything was fine" enabled me to focus on what needed to be on done that day, in that place, at that meeting.

As my husband and life partner, Tom was part of everything I was able to accomplish as president of LLLI. It just wouldn't have happened if he was jealous or upset with my traveling. His reaction was just the opposite, and he would remind me that we could never afford to do that kind of traveling ourselves, "So go and have a good time."

12

An Aura of Integrity

Growing up during the Depression, our family never took vacations. With both sets of grandparents, uncles, and aunts all living in the Chicago area, there wasn't a need to travel to visit family, even if we could afford it. The first real vacation my parents took came after my sisters and I had married, when my mother, father, and my brother Charles drove a few hours away to Springfield, Illinois, to see some of the Abraham Lincoln historical sites.

I really don't remember thinking much about traveling growing up, except for a strong desire to visit Tibet after reading some of the books by Alexandra David-Neel. Born in 1868 in Paris, she was a courageous adventurer who lived in a cave near the Tibetan border for several years to learn spirituality, and later visited Tibet when it was forbidden to foreigners. I could just envision her traveling on horseback through the snowy mountains in Tibet, and I was impressed with her bravery.

So outside of our honeymoon when Tom and I drove to Estes Park in the Rocky Mountain National Park and our summer camping trips with the children in Michigan, I hadn't done any traveling–not even to the Carolina Outer Banks as I'd dreamed. But as president and a co-founder of LLL, all this changed, and I ended up journeying across this country and to close to 40 other countries, meeting people who would enrich my life in a multitude of ways. I found myself speaking in front of an ever-changing array of groups–sometimes side-by-side with doctors who didn't always agree with what I had to say (and vice versa!), sometimes it was LLL conferences, groups of professional women, college students, or the general public. And I was experiencing sights and sounds and tastes that were nothing like anything Tom and I had at home in the unincorporated area of Melrose Park.

My early trips to meetings in this country, and even my first trip out of the country to Canada in 1969, were filled with the kind of stories many travelers tell–of lost baggage, suspicious custom agents, delayed flights, reluctant goodbyes, and then those "Welcome Home, Mom" signs and hugs awaiting me on my return. There were also a few adventures that were not so common–or so I hope, anyway.

"Wait! That's no paved road! That's the *runway!*" My driver was having a problem finding the entrance to a small airport in Florida. Good thing airport security was paying attention and quickly shepherded us off to the side.

A trip to Kansas for a state LLL conference almost ended in a scandal. At the end of the conference, I was brought to a Leader's home to put my feet up and enjoy a drink before leaving to catch my plane. I had just started to sip the whiskey sour she handed me when someone took a look at the clock and realized we were due at the airport "right now." So to be polite, I chugged down my drink, got in the car, and we rushed to the airport. It was too late to check my luggage, so I dashed madly down the concourse, lugging my suitcase. There were no bags on wheels in those days. As I ran through the terminal, the effect of the drink suddenly hit me, and my worry shifted from being afraid that I would miss my plane to worrying that I would collapse flat on the floor, leading to newspaper headlines about the drunken president of LLL and her visit to Kansas!

Those first trips were just preparing me for more exotic adventures to come, such as my early trips to Jamaica and the West Indies. Derrick (Dick) Jelliffe, MD, became my "travel agent" for many of these trips, inviting me to speak at conferences, clinics, and to various professional groups. Dr. Jelliffe, an expert in tropical medicine and infant nutrition, had worked in England, Africa, India, and the Caribbean at that time. He would eventually hold the Chair in Public Health and Pediatrics at the University of California. Although we had been in touch by mail, I didn't meet Dr. Jelliffe until 1970, when he invited me to speak on Young Child Feeding in the Contemporary Caribbean at University of the West Indies in Mona, Jamaica.

Dr. Jelliffe made an interesting remark when he met me at the airplane. "Marian," he said, "as soon as you stepped off the plane, people took one look at you and decided if they were going to believe what you had to say. They take a look at a person and see the aura coming off of them, and then decide if you're to be believed. And if they like what they see and they feel they can trust you, then they come up close to you, so that some of your aura will rub off on them." I'm glad I didn't know that *before* I landed or I would have been afraid to get off the plane!

I was invited to talk about La Leche League and the work we were doing. Arriving at the auditorium, I took a seat in the back of the room, but Dr. Jelliffe asked if I would come and sit up on the stage for the opening talks. So there I was–one woman with seven men, and all of them doctors who were there to talk about breastfeeding.

When the first speaker, a doctor with whom I'd shared the ride from the airport, spoke, I found myself disagreeing–politely, of course–with his recommendation of routine hand expression of milk after each feeding. After my talk another doctor commented that all the points I made were controversial and later described me as "something of a heretic." Imagine– first-born, obedient Marian was now a "heretic"!

My aura must have been in good shape because as a result of that conference, I was invited to a conference of obstetricians in Barbados. That meeting was held in a hospital. It was a very sunny day, and they had huge sliding windows that were kept open, allowing birds to fly in and eat off the trays of patients. During my talk, I started to mention jaundice in the breastfed baby, and quickly realized that they didn't know what I was talking about. So I just shut my mouth, not wanting to export that "problem" to Barbados. Jaundice probably wasn't much of a problem there anyway because it was so sunny. The hospital rooms were drenched in sunlight–similar to the kind of light treatment given to jaundiced babies.

For another talk, I had to take a very small plane into the bush, and I found myself counting the number of stops, as I was told to get off at the third stop. It wasn't really an airport, more like a grassy pasture. My audience consisted of students at a school, and while I was speaking, mothers quietly sidled into the school room, with their babies on their hip or wrapped in a shawl. They were obviously breastfeeding mothers. I pointed out to the students their good fortune at having those experienced women available to help them with breastfeeding when they had babies. It was heartwarming to see the pride in the women's eyes at being honored for what they were doing.

In the 1970's in Jamaica, the formula companies were advertising on billboards and posters all over town. The posters gave the impression that babies would be smarter and grow faster if they were given formula. Of course, there were no billboards describing the benefits of breastfeeding. So it was important to get the word out that breastfeeding was better for babies in every way than feeding formula. I think it helped that this message was being conveyed by an experienced mother of seven breastfed children and not just a strange lady who flew in from another country to tell them what to do. That and having that good aura probably helped, too.

Another talk was at a church filled with mothers and their young babies. The women must have been told ahead of time that there would be a speaker because they arrived in their Sunday best, many of them even wearing pretty hats. Unfortunately, a lot of those dresses opened in the back. And as the babies started to get fussy, obviously wanting to nurse, the mothers were at a loss as to what to do. So I told them that it was fine to nurse their babies in front of me. Opening those dresses from the back and having to pull them down in the front wasn't easy, but one by one the mothers managed to maneuver the neck of their dresses down far enough to make it possible to breastfeed.

Jamaican mothers and their babies filled the church to hear my talk

At a workshop for nurses held at an outdoor stadium, I was talking about the effect of breastfeeding in delaying fertility. One of the nursing supervisors objected, saying "That's what those mothers believe–that if they breastfeed they are not likely to get pregnant." So I asked, "Well, what happens?" And she said, "They don't get pregnant!" but she still thought the idea was nonsense.

My trips to Jamaica and the West Indies were not just about promoting breastfeeding and La Leche League. As rarely happens on my travels, I did get to see the countryside and experience some of the culture first hand. I ate meals with fresh mangoes and pawpaw juice, saw exotic birds from my window, and shared a cottage with a little house lizard, who appeared each morning outside my door and disappeared for the rest of the day.

One free morning I had signed up for a tour of the island. But the tour bus never showed up, and instead Mr. Ashworth, the owner of the hotel, hearing of my dilemma told me that he was driving to his home in Mandeville and would be glad to take me along.

I didn't realize until just then that I had already seen Mr. Ashworth at the hotel and had privately nicknamed him the "British Colonel." He often walked around the hotel wearing a bush jacket, shorts, and white socks, and sported a gray mustache and glasses. I happily accepted his offer, and soon we were on our way.

We drove to Mandeville (altitude 2,000 ft.) where Mr. Ashworth was designing a new hotel and had lunch there–rum punch, pot roast burgundy, and boiled pumpkin. And then we went on to Newport and Mr. Ashworth's home on top of the highest hill for miles around. He had come from South Africa 37 years earlier and planned to go back there to live on a farm with his wife and four children. As he talked about how much he missed them, I could empathize–I was missing my own family so far away.

On the long drive back to Kingston, we passed wild orchids growing on the side of the road. Mr. Ashworth stopped the car and picked some for me, so I had a lovely bouquet. We went through a number of towns and stopped at a small roadside store for fresh orange juice. Mr. Ashworth bought two packages of roasted cashews and two packages of tiny spiced shrimp for us to enjoy. It was a memorable day.

Planning to fly home from Montego Bay instead of Kingston, I decided to take the train through the forest to Montego Bay. I had a first class ticket for a small section in the front of the first car. It was crowded and hot. There didn't seem to be one inch to spare. My luggage sat on the overhead rack– one small suitcase that I could manage easily by myself, and another larger one that was heavy with all the handouts and papers I'd picked up during the conference and meetings.

It was a fascinating ride through the mountains, allowing me to experience the breathtaking views in the forest outside of the city. We passed shanty homes, with women washing clothes in streams, and families bathing in them. At station stops, vendors would come to the windows selling all sorts of food. Then in the middle of the ride, there was an unexpected stop, where we all had to get off the train, while they used our engine to give another train a push. It was a mad scramble and I had to ask a young man to help me get the heavier suitcase down as we got off the train.

When our train returned, it stopped with the door to the first class section right in front of me and my suitcases, and I thought, "Oh, how lucky am I. I can get on first!" Instead I was almost crushed to death, as more experienced travelers climbed over me and around me. Having handed my smaller suitcase to someone through the window, I found it impossible to lift the heavier suitcase up the steps when another man, walking by, just picked it up and carried it on with him. Instead of being the first, I was the last person to reboard the train.

Jamaica and the West Indies are beautiful. But what was I doing there without Tom? It was a question I often asked myself on my trips. Of course, the answer was obvious: Tom had to work and one of us had to be home with the children. Maybe someday we could travel together. In the meantime, I was happy to get back home and into the "mundane" routine of the life I loved. At least until the next trip. . .

13

If it is Good Enough for A Princess

✦

It was my travels in the Caribbean, seeing billboards proclaiming that formula-fed babies grew faster and were smarter, and listening to women who felt that breastfeeding meant they couldn't afford formula, that convinced me of the importance of using celebrities as role models. We needed a woman who could afford any kind of formula, but chose to breastfeed instead, like Princess Grace of Monaco. Famous as Grace Kelly, an award winning actress before she married Prince Rainier of Monaco, she was now the mother of three children.

People around the world were fascinated by the beautiful Princess Grace. Everything the Princess did was newsworthy, including the fact that she had chosen to breastfeed her children.

Hardly anyone believed the Princess would accept our invitation to attend the 1971 LLLI International Conference at the La Salle Hotel in Chicago. But she did! And because her sister, who was to accompany her, was not able to do so, at the last moment I was drafted to be her companion during her stay. Good thing I didn't know about this until she arrived, so there was no time to worry about proper etiquette or clothes. Instead, I found her to be very comfortable to be with. She didn't stand on ceremony, and we spent our down time talking about our home birth experiences and raising our children. She was very concerned with the effect living as royalty might have on her children's lives. We got along so well that we kept in touch and tried to get together on my trips to Europe and her trips to the United States whenever possible.

Receiving line for the Princess

A press conference

The text of the banquet speech Princess Grace gave at our Conference was carried in its entirety by the *Ladies Home Journal*. And in later interviews she gave to magazines like *Vogue* and *Look,* she always mentioned breastfeeding and La Leche League. Her support sent a powerful message about the importance of breastfeeding and had a huge effect on the acceptance of breastfeeding in the United States.

So for a number of years, we continued to feature breastfeeding celebrities like Demi Moore, Susan St. James, Brenda Bixby, Mariette Hartley, and Joan Lunden at our International Conferences and getting to know them as mothers was always a joy. Susan St. James and Natalie Wood even agreed to appear free of charge in "Mother and Child," an instructional film for health professionals that taught me a lot about movie making.

Natalie and her breastfed baby were filmed in the home she and her husband, Robert Wagner, and their children lived in at the time. When we arrived, Natalie asked that the script be written on cue cards, a job that fell to me. I wasn't a particular Robert Wagner fan, but when I heard him come in the door and call out to Natalie, while I was on the floor writing the script on cue cards, I became an instant fan.

When the filming started, Natalie sat on the sofa with her baby on her lap, and I became the cue card holder. This is a much more complicated job than you might expect. The card has to be held at the right angle, and then when the actor finishes with it, the card has to be quietly lowered to the floor, so the noise isn't picked up by the microphone, and another card is held up in its place. This was "on the job" training for me.

Suddenly Robert Wagner came up in back of me. "Natalie, either look at the card or look at the camera," he said, and with that he took hold of one end of the card, and I'm thinking, "Am I really in Natalie Wood's house holding a cue card with Robert Wagner?" It was the kind of strange "who, me?" feeling I would have many times as my life continued to take unexpected turns.

Filming with Susan St. James also held surprises. Susan didn't want to work from a script. She wanted the two of us to be filmed in a park, sitting on the grass, while talking extemporaneously about breastfeeding. Susan's husband at the time, Tom, was a makeup artist. It was a misty day, threatening to turn into rain. During filming when the director would shout, "Cut!" Tom would run over to Susan to fix her makeup and hair. This happened a number of times. There was no one to powder my nose or touch up *my* hair. As the filming went on and my hair got frizzier and my face shinier, I joked that people were going to wonder who that witch was sitting under the tree talking to Susan St. James.

Using breastfeeding celebrities as role models served a purpose in calling attention to breastfeeding and giving it status that was sorely needed. Today, in a refreshing turnaround, it is hard to find a celebrity who will admit to *not* breastfeeding her baby.

14

Globetrotting

It never occurred to me when accepting the role of president of La Leche League that I would be on the road–and in the air–for a good portion of the next 24 years

By the time I was seriously traveling around the world, Philip, our youngest, was in school, and Melanie, our oldest, was in college. And while December-born Sagittarians are supposed to like to travel, I never liked leaving my family. So it was understandable that after talks in Columbia and Argentina one year, I sent this post card from Brazil:

> I gave my last talk at a perinatology conference for Brazilian physicians in a hotel right across from the famous Copacabana beach. The talk went well and I got invitations to visit other Brazilian states, but said "no thank you for now, I want to go home." I'm counting the days…

Shortly after that first trip to Jamaica in 1970, I headed south to Cuernavaca, Mexico. This trip was at the invitation of Ivan Illich, a Catholic priest well-known for his writings about "living small" and his book, *Deschooling Society.* Illich was at once enormously learned and utterly simple in his approach to problems. His proposals shook people up–and made them think.

He had asked me to participate in a discussion of alternatives in healthcare as part of a seminar coordinated by John McKnight, co-director of the Asset-Based Community Development Institute at Northwestern University in Evanston, Illinois. One of the functions of the Institute was to give courses on different aspects of urban life to community workers to make them more effective. The theme that year was: *How do you affect change in a community and improve healthcare without spending a lot of money, just using people in the community?*

The seminar was held at the Center for Intercultural Documentation (CIDOC). Our group of 25 included doctors, sociologists, medical students, nurses, a woman in health insurance, an architect who specialized in hospitals, and me–a mother of seven and president of LLLI!

My days started with a walk up the mountain to the school. This meant that the long days happily ended walking *down the mountain.* It was a beautiful walk, though, through the trees and past waterfalls, and more often than not I found myself confronted by dogs, pigs, chickens, and donkeys. The milk man delivering milk in large cans on the sides of a burro would come by, pouring out the amount of milk requested into a pan provided by the buyer.

The seminar was held outside under the trees when the weather was good or in a large cave if it rained. Students sat on plain wooden benches, unless they got there early enough to stretch out in the rope hammocks, which were suspended in the trees along the perimeter.

On the first day, John McKnight gave the 11:00 a.m. lecture, which was held outside and open to all students to acquaint them with the seminar. That afternoon, it had started raining, and as we walked to the cave for the 3:00 p.m. session, John remembered to tell me that I would be the lecturer that afternoon! Happily, it went quite well. There was a lot of interest in LLL and a number of questions on breastfeeding.

Another interesting speaker was Roslyn Lindheim, an architect from Berkley, California. Roslyn designed pediatric and maternity care facilities, and in her research discovered what I'd figured out years before–that hospitals were not the best place to have a baby. She talked about home deliveries and encouraged discussion as to why couples wanted this kind of experience. Well, it turned out that middle-aged, square Marian, sitting among all those professionals and hippie types, was the *only* person who had had a home delivery. I enjoyed speaking about my experiences, and then answered a lot of questions from the young people in the audience.

It was good for LLL to be represented at this event, and I was so glad to be part of it. Our experience of growing LLL made a unique contribution to the discussion. A number of other organizations learned about us and how they could use our help. It was a valuable experience for me, personally, broadening my thinking about the future development of the League. It gave LLL valuable credibility since Ivan Illich and John McKnight made it clear that LLL was more successful at healthcare–that what we did had better results for improving healthcare in a community–than any other system. They saw that supporting women with breastfeeding can make big changes in the health of a community. This was quite a welcome change to the attitudes we'd seen the year before at that White House conference on Food, Nutrition, and Health!

While at the seminar I even got to go to Acapulco one day, when one of the attendees and his son drove a group of us down to a small secluded beach, where I swam in the Pacific Ocean for the first time. On the way back to Cuernavaca, much to my chagrin, the teenage son drove–through the mountains, in the dark. When the rain started pouring down, we discovered the windshield wipers didn't work. Once the rain stopped, we found ourselves in clouds so thick you could barely see where the narrow two-lane road ended (and the big slide down the side of the mountain began!). This reminded me of my honeymoon trip in the Rockies with Tom years before–but, like Tom, the young driver didn't seem to be in the least bit upset, and we made it all the way back in one piece.

In 1978, Dr. Itsuro Yamanouchi of Okayama, Japan, came to the La Leche League International office to ask if we would send someone to Japan, all expenses paid, to give talks about breastfeeding. As the Chief Pediatrician at Okayama National Hospital, Dr. Yamanouchi was well known through the Japanese media for his support of breastfeeding. The hospital, which included an intensive care center for all premature babies in the region, had the lowest infant mortality rate in Japan during the period when Japan had the lowest infant mortality rate *in the world*. Dr. Yamanouchi insisted that every baby in the hospital receive its own mother's colostrum and milk. If the baby had to stay in the hospital, the mother would be sent home with a breast pump, so she could continue to provide milk for her baby.

I wasn't even present when it was decided I would be the one to go, and I was soon off on what would be the first of three trips I would make to Japan. On this first trip, I was scheduled to speak in three cities to women's groups, LLL Leaders, and health professionals.

Dr. Yamanouchi told me that Japan's new Minister of Health for the government just coming into power was a good friend of his and the father of four young breastfed boys. The Minister's mother was the General Secretary of UNICEF in Japan. Breastfeeding had friends in high places! The *Osaka News* was covering part of my expenses, so we were assured of media coverage. It was a good time to bring attention to breastfeeding.

I found the Japanese to be among the most hospitable people I'd met, with my every need anticipated and taken care of, as I was escorted from one city to another. I got to experience some of the time-honored customs of their culture, which included a communal bath the day I arrived, at which I was the only Caucasian woman present. Somehow it was easier being naked when the other women and I couldn't communicate, and I figured I would never see them again!

My name in Japanese!

My first talk was open to the public and an LLL Leader was my translator. Would the LLL approach to breastfeeding–considered so radical by some in the United States be considered acceptable here? Well, I needn't have worried. As I finished my talk and walked backstage, Dr. Yamanouchi, who was standing there with some other doctors, hugged me and said, "You said exactly what I wanted you to say!" Apparently, I had chosen well. He was so happy–and I was so relieved!

Here I am dressed as a Geisha with Dr. Yamanouchi at my side

I also renewed my acquaintance with Dr. Tatsuo Matsumura, a doctor I had met in India. His work with allergic children convinced him of the superiority of breastfeeding. He also had come to realize that the baby's sensitivity to a particular food often reflected a similar, but unrecognized sensitivity in the baby's mother, and he made the promotion of breastfeeding his life work.

My last night in Japan on that trip, I stayed at the home of an American LLL Leader who was married to a Japanese man, giving me an even deeper experience of Japanese life. We had dinner kneeling at a low table, as usual. Then, as the guest, I was given the honor of first use of the bath water that the rest of the family would later use. Having learned the custom at the communal bath on my first day in Japan, I washed myself off, and then stepped into the vertical tub. That night I slept on a thin mat on the floor. Instead of a blanket, I was given what looked like an ornamental overcoat to slip on with the opening in back. This meant I had to sleep on my back with my head on a pillow filled with buckwheat hulls. So obviously, I was expected to lie still, without tossing and turning. Relaxed by the thoughtfulness and affection of the family and soothed by the sounds of the neighborhood, I did just that.

I also learned another important lesson that evening, although it would have been nice to have learned it earlier. As we got up from the floor after dinner, my hostess who was eight months pregnant told me privately that in her condition she couldn't bear to go through another meal, kneeling at the table. I had faced this problem night after night, kneeling at the table in restaurants in Japan, and told her that when my knees started hurting, I would just change position and sit tailor fashion, with my legs crossed in front of me for the rest of the meal. That's when I learned that in Japan, it was felt that only the most vulgar women sat that way!

When I got home, I told Tom that during my trip, I was taken care of with such kindness that I felt like I was wrapped in cotton. I didn't mention that all the gifts given to me might have been the result of a mistaken perception of my character!

15

Back at the Ranch

What was life like at the Tompson's? This is a question my children were often asked when they were helping out at LLL conferences. And the answer is, "it depends." It depends on a lot of things, including how many children we had at the time, how old they were, and who was being asked.

For example, everybody had a job at dinnertime. It could be mother's helper, setting the table, clearing the table, sweeping the floor, or doing dishes. When we finally got a free-standing dishwasher, we took a picture of Laurel sitting in a chair, reading a book, and "doing the dishes."

The supper job was changed each week, and the initial of each child's first name was written on the blackboard in the kitchen in the order of the job needing to be done. They could also trade jobs with someone else.

On Saturdays, everyone had to clean their portion of their shared bedrooms and a portion of the common area in the house before they could go out and play. There were children who occasionally solved this by putting everything on the floor under their bed, and if I didn't catch it, they were home free. I played records of musicals while we cleaned because I loved listening to them, and it made working more enjoyable.

Our children didn't get allowances. At first, an allowance seemed like a good idea until we realized that eventually we would have to give all seven allowances and that wasn't doable. So we gave them ways of earning extra money instead. In the summer, they could earn 10 cents by filling a shopping bag with weeds. I dispute their claim that the pay for picking dandelions was 100 dandelions for a penny. We lived on a quarter acre lot, so there were a lot of dandelions.

Or they could memorize poetry. We had a large book of collected poems and A. A. Milne's poetry from Winnie the Pooh. I wrote the amount for each poem next to the title. Longfellow's "The Village Blacksmith" was one of the longest poems and worth 25 cents as I recall. Memorizing the Declaration of Independence paid $1.00.

As the oldest child in my family, I was determined to change the kind of responsibility usually expected of the eldest child. So instead, the children were grouped by the color of their hair. Since this ranged from blonde, brunette, redhead, blonde, brunette, redhead, and blonde in that order, it worked quite well. The blondes were responsible for each other, the brunettes and redheads likewise. It was a great way to keep track of everyone, especially when we were out at a museum or the beach.

The Tompson clan

My plan to organize the children this way must have worked because one day Melanie, our oldest, asked me if I was pregnant. We had six children at the time. "No, I'm not expecting a baby," I said. Melanie's response was unexpected. "Darn," she said, "It's getting boring with the same old faces around here all the time."

Speaking of beaches, there wasn't any racial diversity in the suburbs where we lived, so instead of swimming at the suburban beaches, we would take the children to the 12th Street beach on Lake Michigan in Chicago, where they could meet children of many different racial backgrounds. We didn't have air conditioning in our car—or in our house for that matter—but Tom never complained, when after work and eating dinner, we would pile in the car and make the long drive to Lake Michigan.

I used to write a poem for each child's birthday, and then once they were sleeping, I'd hang it above the headboard of their bed, so they would have it first thing in the morning, along with a small "under the bed present" to hold them over until the family celebration at dinner. A number of the children have continued this tradition with their own families. One year, Philip, our youngest, surprised me by reciting several birthday poems from the years before. He also gave me a poem, his first, which nearly 40 years later is still pinned to my bulletin board.

To my mother so dear,

A mother who always lends me her ear.

A mother who's nice and led me through life

And managed very well without much strife.

She is the best, no one is better.

I think an award is what I'll get her.

Love and kisses, Philip

Philip was about seven years old when he wanted to be allowed to hitchhike somewhere for his birthday gift. "Oh Philip," I told him, "We couldn't let you do that. Daddy and I would miss you too much." "But I expected you and Daddy to come along with me," was his response. Philip's perception of "attachment parenting" was even broader than ours!

The only way we could afford a vacation was to go camping, and I loved it! As a former Eagle Scout, Tom was the perfect camping partner. He knew how to do everything. Before we had a camping stove, he made one out of a tin pail, with holes punched in the side. He buried potatoes in the hot coals in the pail, while the meat cooked on a piece of metal screening he would lay on the top. Even when we had a camp stove, he did all the cooking on our vacations.

After "trying out" camping with the borrowed tent of a neighbor one weekend, we bought our own tent. It was a used 16x16 foot canvas army tent, which usually slept a squad of six or eight soldiers. It had a huge center pole that held the tent up, and it was a tribute to Tom's ingenuity that it went up without a hitch, with the help of three little girls and me, standing at each corner of the tent spread out on the ground. As Tom rushed into the tent raising the center pole, we were counted on to immediately tighten the ropes at the corners, and we always did!

The tent not only held our family, the army cots we slept on, and sometimes a buggy, but on rainy days, other children in the campground were welcome to come in and play. The center pole held a circular rod where our Sunday clothes were hung, so we could go to Mass on the way home. After Mass we always stopped for breakfast at a nearby restaurant. It was the one time a year that we ate out as a family, and the only time the children ate out until they turned eighteen. It became a tradition when a child reached eighteen that Tom and I, along with my mother, would take our new eighteen-year-old to a nice restaurant to acquaint the birthday child with the formalities of dining out.

Except for one year when we rented a pop-up travel camper to use on a trip to visit relatives in the southwest, our camping destination was the national forest on top of the sand dunes on Lake Michigan in Muskegon, Michigan. For me, it was a week of freedom, without phone calls or mail, where I was able to just concentrate on the family. When I was pregnant, I had the luxury of lying on my stomach by scooping out a hole in the sand before putting down my beach towel.

There was only one year when we had a problem getting to Muskegon. That was when the Eisenhower Expressway opened in the late 50's, and you had to be able to drive at least 35 miles per hour on the expressway. The car we had that year, loaded with the children inside and the army tent, army cots, and a full size collapsed baby buggy on top, couldn't go that fast!

So we took side roads, playing license plate games in which we would try to find cars from every state or make up phrases using the letters on the plates. And we always did a lot of singing in the car. Several of the girls were in choir at school, and they made us sound really good. The time passed, and we were soon at the campground.

Tom and I divided the chores involved in raising a family. I did the shopping, most of the cooking, and was in charge of the inside of the house. Besides fixing anything that broke, Tom was in charge of the outside. He loved working with the trees and plants. We had a large vegetable garden. Sometimes in the summer, a favorite dinner was simply thick slices of tomatoes and ears of corn. We got to be so "purist" that we wouldn't pick the corn until the water was actually boiling in the pot on the stove. Then we would pick the corn, sit on the step outside the back door while we husked it, and put it in the pot for just a few minutes. It was a fun way to make dinner and so delicious.

Having been a bachelor for so many years, Tom was very comfortable cooking, so on Saturday evening and Sunday morning, he took over.

Saturday's were busy, and we didn't want to have to spend time deciding what to eat that evening, so we always had the same thing: hamburgers, with sliced tomatoes and sliced onions, and baked beans. On Sunday morning, it was eggs and bacon with toast.

Our Sunday morning rituals underwent a change in the late 1960s. Although the Catholic Church had been a big part of my life as a child and young woman, Tom and I found our spiritual lives moving in another direction, and we became members of a newly forming local non-denominational church where we felt in harmony with the teachings. It was a big change, but the right change for us.

Tom was also the science teacher in the family. When we camped, he took the children on nature walks, gathering interesting seeds and leaves. One year, he taught them how to make sundials. Because of Tom, we all learned to find and name the constellations in the sky. When the Russian Sputnik, the first man-made satellite to orbit the earth, was launched, Tom got us all up in the middle of the night, so we could go outside to see when it passed overhead. We became satellite junkies, as more satellites were launched through the years.

Tom brought so much to our family and was incredibly involved in our lives. Even though it was more than 40 years ago, my daughter Deb remembers every detail about how her Dad's expertise and hands-on involvement helped her create science fair projects and wonderful memories:

> When I was in fourth grade, my dad helped me enter the school science fair. We were planning to create an eye that could "see." As impossible as that sounds, we did just that. We purchased a globe of the earth and cut out a circle for the iris. In the back, we had to come up with a retina of some sort. I was bewildered, but Dad had it all figured out.
>
> He had me write a letter to DuPont and ask them for a specific number of ⅛" Lucite plastic rods. When they arrived, it turned out they were seven feet long! Dad got out his hacksaw and cut them in even-sized pieces, and then heated up cooking oil in a cast iron pan. He placed a big bowl of ice water in the sink. On the counter, he had another large pot sitting on its side. Dad heated up the oil and set a 15" length of plastic rod into the hot oil. As it softened, he wrapped the pliable plastic around the lip of the saucepan and plunged it into the ice water. He did this for a total of 36 curved pieces of plastic rod. Then we got two pieces of screening and cut out tiny parts in

such a way that they formed two square grids. We threaded the cut ends of the rods into each of the openings and wound up with a nicely-shaped square grid of curved plastic rods. We hooked up the "retina" to the back of the eye, and shut off the lights. Then I turned on our slide projector and projected a cross, an "X," a circle, and a diagonal line, one at a time into the lens of the eye. Sure enough, the retina "saw" the pattern and transferred it to the "brain," which was the other end of the curved rods.

In seventh grade, we upped the ante. Dad took me around to several department stores and a science store. We bought a ping pong ball, a hand powered iris, and a lens. These all fit together to make the eyeball. Then dad had me write to DuPont again. By this time, things had changed in the science world, and now I asked DuPont for a custom made glass fiber optic bundle. These days, fiber optic bundles are made of flexible plastics, but back then, they were a brand new thing and were made of glass. There were thousands of them, nearly fused together in a bundle about ½" in diameter. I wrote the letter, sent a drawing of a long "J" shape, with specs that I wanted it to meet.

Unbelievably, it arrived in the mail intact. It was again accompanied by a letter from DuPont congratulating me and wishing me well, but there was never a charge. The crude retina and brain we had made a few years before became the Cadillac of retinas and brains. Because there were so many thousands of glass rods transferring light information from the back of the eye to the end of the upturned "J," the picture that the eye could "see" was tiny, but perfectly detailed. When we finished the model with some plaster to hold it all together and some sponge to represent the eye muscles, I entered it, along with my first model, into the state science fair.

I won second place!

———

Christmas came each year with its own Tompson traditions, beginning with the selection of the Christmas tree. Tom was a perfectionist when it came to finding the perfect tree each Christmas. It wasn't unusual for him to go from one Christmas tree lot to another to get the right tree. He had even been known to make a tree from two inferior trees by inserting extra branches from one tree into the other. But one year, when the boys were older, Tom was not feeling well, and he gave Brian and Philip the assignment.

I was making dinner when the boys came home to tell me they had bought a tree, but there wasn't much of a selection. They brought in the scrawniest, most pathetic tree I ever saw. So now I was faced with a dilemma: Could we return the tree? Would Tom have a heart attack when he saw it? And yet I didn't want the boys to feel badly because they did the best they could.

While I was trying to figure out what to do, the boys broke down and told me the tree was a joke, something they picked up on the side of the road. They had bought a perfectly acceptable tree that was in the back yard, but they wanted to play the joke on their dad, too.

So after dinner, we were sitting in the living room, and the boys brought in the pathetic tree to show Tom. Looking over at me, with my head buried and my shoulders shaking, Tom thought I was crying, so instead of getting angry, he decided he would make the best of the situation. He thanked the boys for their diligence, while desperately trying to figure out what he could do to make the tree look presentable. And then, of course, the boys let him in on the joke.

We made our own Christmas cards each year, and it was a family project. Each child would have a particular task to do–gluing on a star, writing the message, etc. Even the youngest child was given something to do.

Christmas Eve began with a procession, with each child holding a figure that was put in the manger. The youngest child came last carrying the Christ Child. Then, with the family gathered around him, Tom would read the story of the first Christmas from the Bible. With the children off to bed, Tom and I decorated the Christmas tree, and then we exchanged the gifts we were giving each other.

Through Sheila's eyes:

> Mom and Dad had a special love for each other. I remember how important the Christmas gifts they would get for each other were to them. My mother would tell us what she was thinking of getting my father, and then ask our opinion. We counted as individuals and what we thought was important. On Christmas Eve, when we were in bed and my parents were exchanging their gifts, we kids would actually be hovered around a heating duct above the living room, so we could hear

their reactions to each other's gifts. It was such a warm and loving feeling listening to them caring so much for each other!

A rare, quiet moment for Tom and I

The children were told they could come downstairs no earlier than 6:00 a.m. the next morning. They would line up in age order, and then come down the stairs and could open just their stocking presents to allow us a little more sleep. Tom and I were typically pretty tired by the time Christmas morning came around—which was somewhat of a mystery until just recently, when Philip finally explained:

> We weren't supposed to come downstairs until 6:00 a.m. by my parents' clock. As the youngest, I was elected to shimmy down the molding of the stairs (so they wouldn't creak), sneak into Mom and Dad's bedroom, and change their clock ahead an hour. It was one of those clocks with numbers that flipped, so I had to quietly flip the time forward without waking them. Sheila and Brian would change the kitchen clock.

No wonder we were so tired!

Our children are all adults now. Most of them have married and started right out parenting their children at a level of consciousness it took Tom and me awhile to reach. They are continuing many of the family traditions they grew up with. Melanie and Deb are now grandmothers, and I delight in watching the joy they find in their grandchildren.

I have found that everything I've put into my parenting has come back to me a hundredfold. It's why, if I had a tombstone, I could have no more meaningful inscription than the exclamation made by Philip one day when we were laughing so hard while playing together that he had to stop to catch his breath and say, "Boy, Mom, I'm sure glad Dad married you."

16

The ABCs of PCBs and DDT

While I might not have had a long formal education, I've never stopped learning. During the years I was at the LLLI office in Franklin Park, there was a period when Dr. Ratner would come in one day a week, and at the end of the day, Dr. Ratner would come sit in my office, and we would talk. We talked about breastfeeding, family life, natural law, and what was going on in the world. It was a custom-made education that was not available at any university, and it made a big difference in the way I viewed the world.

By the late 1960s, La Leche League was considered *the* expert when it came to breastfeeding. That often meant that as LLLI's official spokesperson, I'd find myself on a plane heading to yet another meeting to speak or give testimony on aspects of breastmilk and breastfeeding that went beyond our mission to provide mother-to-mother support. The presence of pesticides and other environmental contaminants in breastmilk was one of these issues.

It wasn't surprising that La Leche League would find itself in the middle of this debate. But it *was* surprising–at least to me–that *I* would be spearheading the campaign. What did I know about complex chemicals whose names I could hardly pronounce? I *did* know breastfeeding, and I *did* know how important breastfeeding was to the world, and that knowledge gave me the impetus to learn what I had to, and speak where our voice needed to be heard.

Studies on contaminants in breastmilk made for attention-grabbing newspaper headlines. Not realizing that this contamination was not just in breastmilk, but in the bodies of everyone living in the same area, mothers were deciding not to breastfeed out of fear–and incomplete information.

By 1970, the public outcry against DDT was growing, and LLLI was being asked as an organization to work towards a ban on the use of DDT. What most people didn't realize was that even scientists disagreed about the potential harm caused by DDT and that attempts to measure DDT in mother's milk, at that time, were questionable at best.

Yet having LLL take an official "stand" against the use of DDT went beyond our mission and good use of our time and money. I did urge mothers in *LLLI News* in 1970 to learn more about this issue and write their elected officials to urge that it be fully explored and resolved.

1976 was the beginning of another contaminant scare: PCBs, or PolyChlorinated Biphenyl, an organic compound used in transformers and coolants that was showing up in breastmilk. We decided to call a meeting in Washington, DC, to bring together scientists, doctors, and other experts to discuss what was actually known and how it might affect breastfed babies. As was becoming all too typical, warnings were going out that were frightening mothers, but there was no real scientific evidence to back up what they implied.

We set our meeting for September 30, 1976, in Washington, DC. Minutes after making this decision, I was surprised to receive a phone call from Dr. Charles Lowe, special assistant for Child Health Affairs, Department Health, Education, and Welfare, inviting me to a meeting they were holding on PCBs in mothers' milk, on September 23, in Washington, DC. I immediately suggested Mark Thoman, MD, a pediatrician on the LLLI Professional Advisory Board and editor-in-chief of *AACTION*, a publication of the American Academy of Clinical Toxicology, as being more knowledgeable on the subject. They wanted both of us to come. Dr. Lowe felt that as a group with a "vested interest," LLLI should be there–and as president, that meant *me*. Within a few days, we had received pounds of background informational material, and as a result, I think LLLI probably had one of the most comprehensive libraries on PCBs in the country.

The first three hours of the seven-hour meeting were devoted to talks on the history of PCB contamination, the bio-medical considerations of PCBs, the levels of PCBs, and human milk sampling and analysis. It was a lot of really technical information about everything *but* why breastfeeding should be protected, with an emphasis on the theoretical dangers of the contamination.

It turned out to be extremely important that Dr. Thoman and I were there to speak about breastfeeding and the effects the scare headlines across the country were having on mothers. In one Michigan hospital, for instance, breastfeeding rates had dropped from 90% to 50% because of the PCB scare!

At the close of the meeting, I publicly thanked DHEW for calling the meeting and showing such concern for mothers and babies, and thanked Dr. Lowe for inviting La Leche League to participate. I also recommended that in any future considerations of this problem, they have as much data on breastmilk and breastfeeding as they did on the possible hazards of contamination. The big scare was cancer, and since immunological and nutritional factors are supposed to play a role in whether or not this develops, eliminating breastfeeding might be just as hazardous, or even *more* hazardous, than the contamination. Dr. David Rall, Chairman of the DHEW Committee to Coordinate Toxicology and Related Programs, agreed that there was a risk-benefit problem. The consensus was unanimous that mothers keep breastfeeding their babies.

The next day, the headline in the *Washington Post* read, "EXPERTS FIND PCBs IN MOTHERS' MILK NOT A PROBLEM." I wondered how many other newspapers would pick up the good news–this kind of headline was not as likely to sell newspapers as those employing the scare tactics!

Nursing mothers can get PBB test kits

Breastfeeding link to PBBs

Breast-feeding scare
Ecologists exaggerating?

Typical environmental pollution headlines from the 1970's

The timing of this meeting was perfect in helping us prepare for our own meeting the next week. I had invited officials from the Department of Health, Education, and Welfare; the Food and Drug Administration; and the U.S. Public Health Service; representatives from environmental activist Ralph Nader's Health Research Group; the Environmental Defense

Fund; the Center for Science in the Public Interest; Griffith Quinby, MD, a founding member of the American Academy of Clinical Toxicology; and several members of the LLLI Professional Advisory Board and Board of Directors. Who would have thought that all of these groups would agree to attend such a meeting called by a *mother-to-mother breastfeeding support* organization? It was truly an indication of the respect La Leche League had earned for itself.

Because this was *our* meeting, we were able to focus on *breastfeeding* and the effect the contaminant scare headlines were having on parents who truly wanted to do what was best for their children. We could speak to all the reasons that breastfeeding should not be so easily dismissed because of the theoretical risk of small amounts of PCBs found in mothers' milk. We could make the case that the immunological properties of breastmilk alone might well offer *protection* from some of the possible effects of contamination exposure, and to remove this source of protection might allow for even greater harm to come to the babies from PCBs. We also pointed out that a baby's exposure to PCB would not just be through breastmilk, but the baby would also be exposed in utero and would continue to be exposed after weaning. It was concluded, again, that there was no reason to discontinue breastfeeding.

The controversy continued, and the next year Dr. Thoman and I were invited back to testify at Senator Edward Kennedy's Sub-Committee on Health and Scientific Research to help dispel some of the anxiety mothers experienced due to these reports of contaminant levels in human milk. Well, to read the reports that came out of that meeting, you would hardly have known we were there. When we read reports of the meetings in the papers and listened to them on TV, it didn't seem like the reporters had read anything we had to say. Media reports were all one-sided and not at all representative of what we'd witnessed at the hearing. An NBC-TV report by Carole Simpson was especially biased, and ended with the statement, "One environmental scientist has suggested that the dangers of breastmilk for children falls somewhere between the dangers of the flame retardant TRIS and saccharin. Based on the evidence, then, if breastmilk were a marketable product, the government would probably have to ban it."

The next day, back in the office, the phone never stopped ringing, as worried parents, the media, and concerned physicians phoned us to find out if we felt that mothers should still breastfeed their babies. We never had such a deluge of calls over a single incident as we had after the reporting of this hearing.

I sent a telegram to NBC protesting the coverage and wasn't the only one to complain. As word spread across the country, Leaders and mothers made phone calls and sent letters by the droves–enough to make NBC follow up on the segment. On June 22, 1977, Jane Pauley discussed the subject on NBC's *Today* Show, interviewing Stephanie Harris and Dr. Joseph Highland of the Environmental Defense Fund and Dr. Art Ulene, each supporting the recommendation that mothers continue to breastfeed their babies. They also pointed out hazards of bottle feeding and that we are *all* affected by environmental contamination.

NBC sent Carole Simpson to Franklin Park to tape an interview with Dr. White, a Leader, and a Leader Applicant, with their nursing babies, and me. At the time, it seemed that Carole was attempting to provide a more balanced coverage based on the questions she asked.

When the segment aired, it showed pictures of the nursing mothers, airplanes dusting crops, and scientists working. It included three sentences from me and a short interview with a doctor who supported breastfeeding. Carole Simpson ended the segment with the remark that "breastfeeding can be considered safe SO FAR!"

I also appeared on the local "AM Chicago" show, speaking again about contaminants in human milk. Sandy Freeman, the co-host was seven months pregnant and said she planned to nurse her baby anyway. Pediatrician and well-known author, Dr. Lyndon Smith, talked about the problems he saw with cow's milk, with both children and adults in his practice. "We're glad to know the figures [on contaminant levels]," he said. "Now, let's forget them."

The simple goal of supporting a breastfeeding mother was becoming a lot more complicated!

17

Becoming Braver

By the 1970s, breastfeeding was making a comeback–and it's reasonable to think La Leche League was responsible for the surge in breastfeeding rates. During 1973, we underwent a growth spurt where three new Leaders were accredited and one new LLL group was forming somewhere in the world *every day!*

That was the year we held our first Breastfeeding Seminar for Physicians. It was something I had been working toward for a couple of years after a local LLL Leader told me how physicians could get credit for attending meetings. Could LLLI put on programs about breastfeeding where doctors could get credit? We found out that before being accredited we had to put on a seminar which the AMA would survey. So I set up a program committee with Doctors Niles Newton, Ratner, White, and Mendelsohn, and in 1973, we put on our first program at Evanston Hospital in Evanston, Illinois.

Although we were only given provisional accreditation at first because of our small budget and use of volunteers, one of the doctors surveying us said, "Even if you aren't accredited, please continue to give these seminars because there is no other place for doctors to get this kind of information." We were soon fully accredited, and from 1973 until 2008, our annual breastfeeding seminars were attended by physicians from all over the world. Reading the evaluation forms, it was obvious the seminars provided a giant step forward in changing the way health professionals perceived breastfeeding and enabled them to better meet the needs of the nursing mother.

One of the speakers at our first Physicians Seminar who became an important gatekeeper for LLL was Derrick Jelliffe, MD, an expert in infant malnutrition. Dr. Jelliffe was working in Africa when he heard about La Leche League at a conference in Hawaii. He immediately sent for all our material, which would then be read over the radio. Most families in Africa had transistor radios, and it was a useful tool for providing information on breastfeeding.

Wait a minute. Mothers in Africa needed our help to breastfeed? I was in the habit of telling moms at meetings that if they lived in Africa, breastfeeding would be easy and considered natural. What I didn't realize was that widespread advertising by formula companies had women questioning the value of breastfeeding and striving to give their babies formula.

The reach and cleverness of the formula companies became quite clear when Dr. Jelliffe asked me to give a talk on the influence of women's groups on infant feeding trends at the 15th International Congress of Pediatrics held in New Delhi, India, in 1977. The theme of this conference was "Every Baby Deserves to be Breastfed."

There were colorful billboards posted around the city with slogans like, "Our Birthright—Mother's Milk" and "Babies Bloom on Mother's Milk." But it became sadly evident to me while talking with some of the 4000 physicians attending from around the world, that while they might be in favor of breastfeeding, they had little understanding of how it worked. Typical was the doctor who told me that the babies in his practice refused to suck. The fact that this might be happening because the mothers in his practice did not get to breastfeed until 24 hours after birth and after the baby had several bottles had never occurred to him.

Most of the sessions took place in a large auditorium, with exhibitors arranged along the walls on the sides and back of the room. A prominent formula manufacturer had the brilliant idea of giving away beautiful, oversized Indian prints in large rectangular envelopes, with the name of the company printed in huge letters across the back. As I sat at the panel and looked out over the audience, I could see a sea of envelopes with the name of the formula company staring back at me, as the doctors, sitting with the envelopes clasped to their chests, listened to the talks. Obviously, they didn't realize that by carrying those large envelopes around at a conference about breastfeeding they had become unpaid advertisers for a formula company.

Maybe it was because I felt a bit intimidated as the only non-professional speaker on the panel, that I didn't say anything. I didn't want to embarrass Dr. Jelliffe, who was moderating the panel, by causing a stir, so I kept quiet. In retrospect I wish I'd been braver and pointed out the irony of that moment. But I didn't.

My Mom and I at the Taj Mahal

The formula companies must have recognized LLL was a force to be reckoned with. Two years later, I received a call from the president of that same formula company. He said that La Leche League had done a magnificent job of increasing breastfeeding rates, and he wanted to help us get a good affirmative action program going in Third World countries to encourage breastfeeding. There was an international meeting planned that fall in Switzerland, where participants would be discussing a possible code of ethics for formula marketing. He despaired of this code being productive, saying that his company had been working on one for nine years, and he wanted to help facilitate LLL's coming forward with a practical program for breastfeeding.

He said we should set up a training school and get an executive to manage it. "Good management makes good movements. You don't have to have us involved in any shape or form—we could help get money out of Congress." He said there will be another billion people on this earth in the next 11 years, so poverty will be worse in the next ten to 20 years. He surprised me by noting that as breastfeeding increased, so did their formula sales. He said that La Leche League made women so nutrition-conscious that they were more likely to purchase formula instead of using regular cow's milk if they decided to bottle-feed. He offered to get us several million dollars through Congress, so we could set up breastfeeding programs on six continents. Surprisingly, he admitted that even if the formula company's name was not used in connection with the money, people would know they had made it possible and would have better feelings about them.

I said very little during the conversation, which I am sure was supposed to impress me. I mostly listened and thanked him for calling. Then I talked to Dr. Jelliffe, who had a long history of conversations with formula company executives. He said that with the WHO/UNICEF meeting coming up on the ethics of formula marketing, the formula companies were out to white-wash themselves. I was sure that whoever would be representing that formula company at the WHO/UNICEF meeting the next month would like very much to announce they were aiding La Leche League in setting up breastfeeding programs.

Shortly after, I was invited to a round table discussion with members of the medical community on counseling the breastfeeding mother, sponsored by the same formula company. I was not asked to speak, but was told I could join in the discussion afterwards.

I knew and respected some of the people who would be speaking, but all my instincts and prior experiences were waving red flags and saying, "No!" Some of the LLLI Board Members and other founders felt LLL should participate. Dr. Jelliffe, however, was very suspicious of their motivation. "When you stand next to a formula company," Dr. Jelliffe used to say, "you make them look good and you look bad."

I also realized that publicity on LLL's participation could be used by the formula company in any way they wanted to use it. So, just as I turned down their offer to get LLL "millions of dollars" from the US Congress, I also declined this invitation.

It was just as well. I heard later from a friend who did go that it was a waste of time, and incredibly, among the issues discussed at the meeting was how to help a mother break away from an over-zealous LLL Leader. Obviously, we were friends no longer!

By 1979, worldwide awareness of the effect formula marketing was having on breastfeeding and infant health was intensifying. A joint WHO/UNICEF meeting on Infant and Young Child Feeding was convened in Geneva, Switzerland. I had been invited to attend, but learned there would be no mothers from developing countries present at the meeting, and so I offered to have LLL undertake a survey of mothers in developing countries with the help of our League Leaders. This would give everyone a more detailed background on breastfeeding practices in those countries.

We received many thoughtful replies from women in the Ivory Coast, Kenya, El Salvador, Columbia, New Guinea, Mexico, and other countries. They all told of similar problems, which included getting incorrect information from healthcare professionals.

A second meeting on Infant and Young Child Feeding was held a few months later, and because the non-governmental organizations (including LLLI) were allowed to have two representatives present, I invited a League Leader living in Geneva, who, along with her physician husband, was very interested in the issue.

It was a good session. Some of the additions suggested to the first draft of the Code were that literature from formula companies not only show the superiority of breastfeeding, but also the hazards of bottle feeding and that formula-feeding can be hazardous, even when instructions for its use are followed. At the first meeting, I had asked that this kind of information be put on the formula cans, but the suggestion received no support. The group wanted full disclosure when formula companies underwrite research projects or sponsor doctors' trips to conferences. A strong stand against free gifts to doctors and free supplies to hospitals was taken.

The next day, I was invited to a meeting of the newly established International Baby Food Action Network (IBFAN), where its purpose of monitoring formula marketing and lobbying was discussed.

I'd come a long way from that meeting in India where I was uncomfortable speaking up when I saw doctors falling prey to the marketing practices of formula companies. Little by little, given so many opportunities, I was finding my voice and getting braver.

18

"Truth Must Dazzle Gradually"

Looking back over the conferences and meetings I attended in those whirlwind years in the late 1970s, it is interesting to see how many of the ideas about breastfeeding that we take for granted today were at one time considered radical. In 1976, I was invited to Strasbourg, France, to speak at the "Symposium on Non-Cancerous Breast Diseases." This was an unusual and progressive look at possible connections between breast disease and the absence of breastfeeding. While the protective effect between breastfeeding and cancer prevention had been acknowledged in the early 50's, this had somehow fallen out of favor. But now more studies were coming out, suggesting a deterrent effect between breastfeeding and breast cancer.

On the Swiss leg of that trip, I met a doctor who was the head of the Obstetrics Department at his hospital. He was very excited about a new tool they were using, ultrasound, to monitor labor. I asked him, "How do the women feel about being confined to their beds and having that strap around their bellies during labor?" I couldn't imagine that such a device would have been something I would have liked. The doctor replied, "Oh, it's fine. Why don't you come to the hospital tomorrow morning and you can see for yourself?"

The next morning I went to the hospital and became "Dr. Tompson"–complete with an official white coat–and we headed into the room where a woman was laboring with the ultrasound strapped in place. "Mrs. Smith, how are you?" the doctor asked. She replied, "Oh, Doctor, this is terrible! I can't move around. I have to stay in bed. I hate it!" So much for women being "fine" with it! It reminded me of another woman I'd heard about who was in labor with the ultrasound in place. Everybody in the room was glued to the monitor, and all of a sudden the heartbeat stopped, and they all gasped, sure something horrible had happened. What had happened was the baby had been born right there on the bed! The reason there was no heartbeat on the monitor was because the baby was no longer inside!

Following the WHO/UNICEF meeting on Infant and Young Child Feeding in Geneva, my mother and I flew to Italy, where I was to give seven talks in six cities over five days, along with the usual TV, radio, and newspaper interviews, as well as private discussions with health administrators. The credit for setting up this "tour de force" went to Shanda Bertelli, daughter of Bill Lear of Lear jet fame. Shanda handled all the scheduling, and she also accompanied my mother and me every step of the way, acting as an interpreter when needed. This trip was special for both mother and me because we were able to include short visits with family in Forli and Bologna. These were relatives I had never met.

My mom and I on a train in Italy

The invitation to Italy came as a result of a mysterious and often fatal malady that had afflicted hundreds of babies the previous year. Research finally revealed that the "Evil Disease," as it was called, was actually seven different respiratory diseases, and significantly, no deaths occurred among babies who were totally breastfed. Deaths were higher among bottle-fed babies than among babies who received both bottle and breast. When the cause of this problem was finally identified, I found a study in our LLL files which indicated that breastfeeding was a great protection against this kind of virus. So I wrote to Shanda, a LLL Leader in Milan, asking if she could get this study into the hands of someone in authority there. We were able to also offer her financial assistance to be used in reprinting some of our pamphlets in Italian.

That the work of the LLL Leaders in Italy was highly respected was obvious in the introduction Professor Giorgio Giovannelli, Director of the Pediatric Clinic at the University of Parma, gave me to a group of several hundred physicians: "We have known about the advantages of breastfeeding for a long time," he said, "but these women have actually been able to do something about it. We should listen to them."

In Naples, our talk was sponsored by the Health Department and, unbeknownst to me, had been advertised with 25,000 posters circulated throughout the city, as part of a breastfeeding campaign. It was in Naples that most of the babies had been taken ill.

My talk was held in a castle on the bay of Naples. The posters had done their job, and the room was packed. People were even standing outside leaning in the windows! During my talk, with Shanda instantly translating, I asked if anyone in the audience had nursed a baby. One woman, who had nursed for three months, raised her hand. "Okay. You can be the first resource person for your community!" I said and invited her to the front of the room, where I introduced her to the crowd.

Standing in front of the Castle on the Bay of Naples

One television interview on that trip makes me chuckle every time I think about it. I don't know exactly where we were, but a physician picked my mother and me up and drove us to a small square building that housed a TV station. We walked inside while a Laurel and Hardy movie, with a voice-over in Italian, was playing. The doctor and I were told to sit down on two chairs facing each other and a young man, the cameraman, came in with what looked like a box camera on legs. Immediately, Laurel and Hardy were turned off, and the doctor and I started talking live. In the back of my mind, I could visualize angry Italians complaining about what happened to the show they were just watching! When our discussion ended, Laurel and Hardy went back on the air, and we were out of there before any angry viewers could show up!

February 1980 brought yet another overseas trip, this time to the Israeli Pediatric Society's International Symposium on Breastfeeding in Tel Aviv. Because of my experience in putting on breastfeeding seminars for physicians, Dr. Serem Frier, Chairman of the Conference and President of the Israel Pediatric Society, asked for my help with planning the program.

He also invited me to give a talk. Arriving at the hotel in Tel Aviv, I headed to the cocktail party and met with League mothers and LLL Leaders, as well as a "who's who" in breastfeeding at the time—Doctors Lawrence Gartner, Itsuro Yamanouchi, Paul Fleiss, Armond Goldman, and others, many of whom had significant connections to LLL. It was a happy gathering of people, excited at seeing each other and eager to catch up on all that was going on.

The next day the symposium began with a keynote address by Otto Wolfe of the University of London on "The Place for Breastfeeding in the Medical Student Curriculum." His rather scientific pro-breastfeeding talk included the interesting remark that watching a breastfeeding mother and baby may reawaken in medical students some of the compassion that is often lost during their medical training. That first day, there was only one mother and nursing toddler present. They had flown in all the way from Australia for the meeting. Dr. Arthur Eidelman of Jerusalem, chairing the first session, made the announcement that there was to be no smoking in the auditorium, but breastfeeding was allowed.

The papers the first two days were mostly scientific. We heard from Barbara Hall of London, who spoke on the difference between foremilk and hindmilk. Dr. Gerald Gaull, known for his research on taurine, made the remark that while taurine is very low in cow's milk, it is lower still in cows used for chronic milking. He ended his talk with the remark by Emily Dickenson that, "Truth must dazzle gradually or every man be blind." Dr. Eidelman spoke from "my bias" that it is quite clear that the milk of mothers of pre-term infants meets the need of pre-term infants, and he went on to state that he felt the feeding of pooled mother's milk was just as artificial as cow's milk. We heard about allergies, early solids, and bacterial colonization of pumped milk.

By mid-week, the focus shifted from research to how to help mothers' breastfeed, and how to bring the message to the community. LLL Leaders and their babies, along with other women who worked with breastfeeding mothers, arrived to listen to the talks. They sat very quietly in the back of the room, moving out with their babies whenever the babies started to get noisy. But it was obvious, looking at many of the scientists there, that they were not used to such distractions. Many had never heard a live baby in a meeting before and would turn and glare when a baby made any kind of noise.

During the morning break, Dr. Frier got up to announce that they didn't realize there would be so many babies present, so they had secured a room on the third floor with a sitter to watch them, so the mothers could leave their babies and listen to the talks. At the end of the coffee break, ushers were quite sternly telling mothers with their babies that they should not be in the room. I was standing in back with the mothers and knew that something had to be done and the best time to do it would be during my talk, which would take place right after the break. "Stay where you are," I told the mothers, "I will take care of it," as my mind whirled crazily wondering what I could do.

I must explain that this was a very formal meeting–speakers had to submit papers ahead of time, and each speaker was given a specific amount of time to talk. One minute before their time was up, a warning light on the podium would come on, and a minute later, the microphone was turned off.

Walking up to the podium, I felt my disguise fall away. Up until that moment I had been treated like a colleague, a doctor–they often called me "Dr. Tompson"–and they were about to find out I was just a mother. I knew I had to change the beginning of my talk, even though the translators in the booths at the back of the room would be frantic trying to figure out what happened. I started out with a word of appreciation for the scientific papers that had already been given and suggested that as a result of hearing these papers, a lot of people present were more enthused than ever about breastfeeding and would like to use some means of helping mothers to breastfeed their babies. Then to soften them up, I told them that in the United States we used a Madison Avenue approach and brought out "Tru Breast"–a satirical flier on breast vs. bottle written by a LLL Leader that listed such attributes as nipples that don't fall on the floor, so they don't have to be sterilized; milk containers that are decorative even when not in use; etc. So the doctors were laughing. That's good, I thought.

Then I spoke of my reason for being there, to talk about the differences between breastfeeding and bottle-feeding–differences many young mothers are not prepared for when they decide to breastfeed. Just as their experience of motherhood would be different from that of the bottle-feeding mother, so were the problems and concerns that might confront them. Calling attention to the generous offer of the Conference Committee of a room for the babies at the Conference, I noted that this kind of offer could only be made in a society where bottle-feeding was the customary way of feeding a baby, and where caretakers for the infant were thought to be interchangeable. This would not happen in a breastfeeding culture, I said, because there, mother and baby would be considered a unit; the baby, feeling the mother was part of him, and the mother feeling like the baby is part of her. And knowing that her baby missed her, the mothers would find it hard to concentrate on the talks. I was sure that the scientists who presented the papers the past two days wanted to see their research translated into mothers actually breastfeeding their babies. The mothers present with their babies were the volunteers who would help other women breastfeed their babies. "While baby noises can be distracting, I am sure these mothers will make every effort to not let it interfere with your listening. And if a particular mother does not seem to notice that her baby is making noise, I am sure she will not be offended if she is reminded of this. But we do need each other."

Once it was pointed out, they understood.

Then I went on to give my prepared my talk, which incidentally was entitled, "Meeting the Needs of the Breastfeeding Mother and Baby," when it occurred to me that I'd been talking for quite a while and had no idea how much time remained. There were some points I wanted to be sure to cover. So I turned to the Chairman, Dr. David Baum of Oxford, England, and said, "I'm not sure how much time I have left and hope you can tell me." And Dr. Baum responded, "We wouldn't dare stop you, Mrs. Tompson! We didn't even set the timer. You can talk as long as you want." So I finished with the thoughts still needing to be said and brought my talk to a close soon afterward. There was no time for questions, but a nurse-midwife from National Childbirth Trust in England got up to say that the National Childbirth Trust endorsed everything I had said.

As we walked out for lunch, Dr. Serem Freier, instead of being offended by my remarks, invited me to have lunch with him, Dr. Gerrard, and Dr. Richard Deckelbaum of Jerusalem. The four of us became a committee to draw up resolutions that the other participants could then vote on. I suggested that we use the recommendations of the joint WHO/UNICEF meeting as our guide and we did. The recommendations included education on breastfeeding for boys and girls, as well as medical and nursing students, good nutrition for the expectant mother, support of the husband, nursing as soon as possible after delivery, discouragement of supplementary feeds, and nothing but breastmilk for the first four to six months. These recommendations were passed out to the participants the next day, and although we never had a formal vote on them, Doctor Freier planned to bring them to the attention of the Israel Pediatric Society, so they could endorse the statement, and then bring it to the International Pediatric Congress, which would be held in Spain later that year.

One last note about that day's program, there was no problem about my title or lack of one as Dr. Baum began introducing me as "The High

Priestess of Breastfeeding Mothers," and that is how I was referred to during the rest of the meeting.

Friend of the Court—and Nursing Mothers

In the 1970s and 1980s, breastfeeding mothers were being attacked from all angles. We had environmental scares, misleading formula marketing, and legal battles. Just as health professionals were turning to LLL as the authority on breastfeeding, mothers finding themselves involved in the court system were also seeking our help. And once again, I found myself a participant in something totally new to me: writing legal briefs and *testifying* in court!

These legal situations generally fell into one of four categories: visitation after a divorce, nursing in public, work-related issues, and jury duty. It was a divorce case that got me started. While lawyers rightly guard the rights of divorced parents in building relationships with their children, they typically viewed breastfeeding as just another way of getting food into the baby. Bottles could easily be substituted when Dad had a weekend with the baby. While the visit with Dad might seem fair to a judge, it meant emotional and physical upheaval for Mom and baby. Mothers, desperate to find credentialed professionals to provide information to the court on why breastfeeding mattered, turned to La Leche League.

The attorneys engaged in working out visitation with a breastfed baby welcomed any information we could provide. So I became an *amicus curiae*—"friend of the court"—a volunteer who offers information to help the court understand the issues at hand. I created an amicus brief with articles and letters from professionals that spoke to the importance of breastfeeding and the problems that occurred when it was interrupted.

As breastfeeding became more common, so did the uproar caused by mothers nursing their babies in public. There was the mother who lost her swimming pool membership when, covered by a large beach towel, she nursed her two-month-old at the side of the toddler pool, while she kept an eye on her toddler. This mother and I were invited to appear on a number of TV shows to discuss what some considered outrageous behavior. Other mothers were asked to leave restaurants or nurse babies in the restroom. Even the famous became targets.

In 1976, Margaret Trudeau, wife of Canadian Prime Minister Pierre Trudeau, nursed her baby in public, resulting in unfavorable publicity for her. While in Ontario to do a live TV talk show, the first question I was asked was what I thought of Margaret Trudeau breastfeeding in public. Although the interviewer had breastfed her own child and was in favor of breastfeeding, she didn't think a mother should nurse in public. I replied that while mothers can nurse their babies rather unobtrusively, if the mother is Margaret Trudeau, everybody is going to be watching her, so it would be almost impossible for *her* to nurse unobtrusively. Yet she was doing the most important thing a mother can do and that was tending to the immediate needs of her baby. I remembered being in a similar situation myself while having lunch at a restaurant in Chinatown in San Francisco. With an older baby, nursing unobtrusively is not always easy. Thank goodness I did not have to deal with photographers at the same time!

The cases that involved working mothers not only involved convincing employers of the value of breastfeeding, but they also often created challenges for normal workday routines and procedures. One year I was asked to testify in Milwaukee for a teacher who was going to lose her job because she asked to stay home with her nursing newborn two weeks beyond her maternity leave, which would run right into summer vacation. The school wouldn't allow it. The teacher's rationale was that she would have been given the time off, as other teachers had, if someone in her family was sick or if she were taking classes for her education. Being allowed to take an extra two weeks off, so as not to interrupt breastfeeding until summer vacation started was important, too. So Dr. Mendelsohn and I were asked to defend the importance of breastfeeding at a hearing which was conducted very much like a regular courtroom procedure. Both the hearing officer and the school's lawyer were women, but they were not impressed by the evidence for breastfeeding. And while the teacher lost her case and left the school, her intent was to also prevent other breastfeeding teachers from being treated so unfairly in the future. On that point she succeeded. Her case became a catalyst. Not wanting to undergo more unfavorable publicity, the school superintendent saw to it that the rules were changed to be more helpful to teachers who were breastfeeding their babies.

The case of one working mother, Linda Eaton, a firefighter in Iowa, gained national attention for breastfeeding and La Leche League. Linda, a single mom, was suing the Fire Chief after she was suspended for breastfeeding her baby in the seclusion of the women's locker room at the fire station during her free time.

This was 1979, and there were few woman employed as firefighters. Linda was the only female firefighter in her particular fire station. After her baby was born, she had a maternity leave of three months because of health problems. As was required, she went to the city doctor before returning to work and told him that she intended to continue breastfeeding her baby during her free time at the firehouse. The doctor then phoned the Director of Human Resources, and told her of Linda's intent to breastfeed. The Director called the Fire Chief and said, "What are you going to do about it?" The Fire Chief, maybe feeling pressured, immediately said he would not allow it.

The city council then passed a resolution that no one could breastfeed in the firehouse. In the meantime, Linda was pumping milk for her baby to be given when she was away. Linda's work shift was 24 hours on the job, 24 hours off, 24 hours on, 24 off, 24 on the job, and then four days off. The baby had no formula, and on her first day back at work her sister brought the baby to her at noontime to nurse.

The Fire Chief sent a woman down to see if she was breastfeeding, and although the baby was covered with a blanket, Linda was suspended for the rest of the day. On her second day of work, her sister brought the baby in, and they went through the same charade, with her being suspended and not getting paid. At this point, Linda was not only hurting financially, but she was losing weight due to the tension.

In the meantime, at the LLLI office, we were getting phone calls from the media asking if we were really supporting Linda and why. We found this an excellent opportunity to educate a lot of people not only about the difference between breastmilk and formula, but also between breastfeeding a baby and giving that baby breastmilk in a bottle.

During this time, Linda's baby had not taken more than a few drops of milk from a bottle, even though it was breastmilk. Instead he preferred to wait until his mother came home–a practice not uncommon for breastfeeding babies who have to be separated from their mothers. On the third day, when Linda's mother brought the baby to the firehouse, a fire alarm came while Linda was in the midst of nursing Ian. Linda was the second person on the truck and when the fire truck arrived at the scene, she was the first person inside the burning house. This was all recorded by television and newspaper reporters.

Her lawyer phoned me on a Saturday and asked if I would be willing to be in Iowa to testify on Monday morning at 9:00 a.m. They had found a doctor who would testify to the importance of breastmilk, but after talking to him, the lawyer realized that he wasn't all that enthusiastic about breastfeeding.

I offered to file an amicus curiae brief on the importance of breastfeeding with the Court. Since the American Academy of Pediatrics and the American Medical Association had both come out with statements encouraging breastfeeding that year, I decided to get in touch with both organizations, asking them to join with us in the brief. Dr. Mendelsohn knew the Vice President of the AMA and offered to phone him. In return he received a lengthy phone call from an AMA lawyer, explaining why they could not support Linda.

I talked to a spokesperson for the American Academy of Pediatrics, who said they were just not equipped to handle these kinds of requests.

On Sunday evening, I learned that the lawyer had just come out of nine hours of discussion with the Fire Chief and the City Manager. When they finally reached an agreement, the lawyers for the city said the Fire Chief and City Manager had no authority to make an agreement, and so it was not binding. The judge asked that the list of witnesses be held down at the hearing, so I would not have to go to Iowa after all, and our amicus brief wasn't necessary.

At the end of the hearing, Linda's injunction against the Fire Chief was upheld. She could continue to breastfeed her baby, while the Civil Rights Commission investigated the matter. The judge in his closing remarks spoke eloquently of what Linda was trying to do as a mother.

The reaction to this case was interesting. We received letters from people upset with our support of Linda's efforts. I am sure some of them were because of press stories, which gave the impression that she was a liberated woman who was just trying to make a test case, and others objected to our support of a single mother. Phil Donahue invited Linda on his nationally syndicated television talk show and asked me to be there with her. It was an interesting show, where the initial hostility of some of the women in the audience evaporated by the end of the show. But the anger was still present in the phone call I got when I returned to the office. "I've donated money to LLL for years," the voice on the other end started out, "but if you are going to defend an unwed mother, I'm not giving you another cent." "I totally agree with you," was my response, "if you believe that babies born to single mothers should not be allowed to breastfeed, then you should not support us because La Leche League will continue to help every mother who wants to breastfeed her baby." There was silence and then a dial tone.

Phil Donahue, Linda with her baby, and me

Ultimately, the Iowa Civil Rights Commission awarded Linda's legal fees and damages, stating that she had been the victim of sex discrimination. She was allowed to have her son brought to her for feedings. She left her position when Ian was 16 months old. A few months earlier, she described her motives in a letter to the editor of *Iowa Woman*:

> It's important for people to understand why I did not just quit my job, or put my baby "on the bottle." The reasons were a simple combination of my need for employment, my feelings for the firefighter job that I was just barely getting a look at, and my sincere, intense, motherly instinct. That instinct told me to give my son the best, healthiest, most secure bond with which to begin his life–the bond between the nursing couple.

Today it is not uncommon for nursing mothers to be firefighters. In fact, I've met an LLL Leader whose firefighter daughter is in charge of distributing breast pumps to the breastfeeding firefighters in her district. And it only took 30 years!

20

Lights! Camera! Shyness, Be Gone!

Add to the long list of things I never imagined I would be doing–appearing on television. We already had three children when Tom, who worked at Zenith Radio Corporation, built our first television set. Years later, I would be actually appearing on a wide variety of television shows, both here and abroad.

I remember the first time all too well. It was a local Chicago TV show, the *Jim Conway Show*, in 1961. The letter had said, "Dear Mrs. Tompson, We look forward to your participation on the *Home Telecast*. . . ." I'd seen this show before where a panel of guests sat at a table, and the camera would pan to each person's face as they were introduced. How hard could that be! But as my name was read and the camera focused on me, I couldn't even move my mouth to smile. It was frozen. I couldn't make the corners of my mouth budge. I'd seen Jackie Gleason do a comedy routine like this on TV once, but it wasn't funny this time. And my heart was beating so loudly, I just knew people must be hearing it through the mike clipped to my dress. *Tha-thump, tha-thump, tha-thump...!* I guess it must have gone well enough, though, as I was asked back on that show a number of times.

The *Phil Donahue Show* was still being televised in Dayton, Ohio, where it originated, when LLL Leaders there wrote to Phil Donahue in 1969 and suggested he have me on the show. Not only did he invite me, the local Leaders were invited to be in the audience. This meant their babies came along, too. It was the first time babies were ever allowed in the audience on the *Phil Donahue Show*. Phil and I hit it off, and I ended up appearing on his show six times. When his autobiography, *My Own Story*, came out, he sent me a copy. I don't think I was mentioned in the book–nor did I expect to be–but I did recognize a phrase he'd used to describe me on that very first show in Dayton. At one point, he had me stand up and said, "This lady could sell me a dead rat." So it was sort of funny in the book to see him describe his father as someone who could sell you a dead rat. We must have been two of a kind!

Phil Donahue's shows reached millions of viewers and changed many lives. One that I heard about first hand was from an LLL Leader I met at a conference. "How did LLL come into your life?" is a favorite question of mine, and it's what I asked her. "Well, I had just come home from the doctor with my baby," she replied. "My doctor told me that I had to stop breastfeeding. I was so disappointed that once home I couldn't stop crying. So I turned on the TV to distract myself, and there you were with Phil Donahue, talking about breastfeeding and La Leche League. I immediately found an LLL Leader, was able to keep nursing my baby, and now I'm a Leader, myself, helping other breastfeeding moms." Thank you, Phil Donahue.

Breastfeeding was a new topic, and radio and TV shows looking to fill up time were quick to look to us for something different. Here, for example, are my notes on a weekend one September: "On the evening of the 28th I flew to Detroit, where I was picked up by a local Leader and taken to the Southfield Sheraton Hotel. The next morning at 4:15 a.m. Chicago time I had to get up to do a live *Good Morning, Detroit* TV show. This was followed by another live *This Morning* TV show, immediately followed by a radio interview. Then back to the hotel where I addressed a luncheon for doctors and nurses. That evening I gave a public lecture in the hotel ballroom attended by some 250 people. The next day was spent attending and speaking at the Detroit Area LLL Conference." It was a hectic, but fruitful weekend, and not all that uncommon.

Sometimes I was put on the spot. In the 1970's, pediatrician Dr. Barry Brazelton and I were invited to appear on the nationally broadcast TV show, *Not For Women Only*, hosted by Barbara Walters, a well known American broadcast journalist and author. At one point during the discussion about meeting the needs of our children, Barbara asked me directly, "How long did you breastfeed?" Not wanting to shock her, I said, "Past a year." Barbara wouldn't let it end there, "No, EXACTLY how long did you breastfeed?" So I told her the truth. My son Philip, the youngest of our seven children, was four when he weaned. Noting the stunned look on Barbara's face, Dr. Brazelton immediately jumped into the breach and said, "Oh, that's common around the world. That's not unusual at all!" I loved him for saying that!

I'd come a long way from that first terrifying appearance on the *Jim Conway Show*. I still was concerned about not letting the Leaders down, but I could at least relax enough to smile in front of the camera. Shyness, be gone! After all, this wasn't about me, it was about breastfeeding, and though I was always a little nervous, we couldn't have been luckier being given so many exciting opportunities to talk about it. Slowly but surely breastfeeding was infiltrating a culture that was not quite sure what to do with it.

Partings

My husband Tom's death in 1981 was totally unexpected.

Even though he was older than me, Tom had such a strong constitution I always felt he would outlive me. But he was hit by a car as he walked down the road outside our house.

It had been a rainy November evening. Tom wanted to buy some ice cream, so as soon as the rain stopped, he started to walk to the little grocery store at the end of the street. There were no sidewalks where we lived. It was dark and misty after the rain. Tom was walking on the side of the road, but apparently stepped out around a puddle in the road just as the young boy who lived down the street drove by. Our son, Philip, was leaving to take Tosh, our Dalmatian, out, and we were in the doorway talking when we heard the car hit something. It was Tom.

When the paramedics arrived from the fire station, I was glad to see that my cousin George was among them. I wasn't allowed in the back of the ambulance while the paramedics worked on Tom, but George was there, family was there to explain what happened when he woke up. After what seemed like an hour, Tom hadn't regained consciousness, and we were off to the hospital where they worked on Tom some more. Finally, George came out of the emergency room to tell me that Tom was gone. I appreciated that it was a family member who hugged me as he gave me the news, and I was so grateful I was right there and not out of town when the accident happened.

Brian, who was in college, and Philip, who had just graduated from high school, were still living at home, and they called the other children with the sad news.

The next day when I called the neighborhood funeral director, I already knew I wanted Tom's wake and funeral to be at home. He had been taken away too quickly. I remembered when Tom's stepfather died a few years earlier how the children didn't like leaving Grandpa Tompson's body alone in the funeral parlor at the end of the day.

"We don't do wakes at home anymore," the funeral director explained over the phone. "Those haven't happened for 30 or 40 years."

"I'll be right over," I responded, "and we can talk in person."

And drawing on what I'd learned during many years of being in the minority, whether it was about childbirth or breastfeeding or other situations affecting our family, I walked into the funeral home surrounded by my sons and sons-in-law, many of them well over six feet tall. There is safety in numbers.

I sat down with the men around me, and I explained the reason for my request. "We are a very home-oriented family. We have our babies at home, our daughters have been married at home, and I would like my husband's wake to be at home." Then I just sat quietly. There was no more to be said. It was obvious that I couldn't be persuaded otherwise, so at the risk of losing the business, or perhaps because he was sympathetic to our plight, the funeral director agreed.

A night out with Tom

Tom came home in a casket, which was put in the living room in front of the bookcase that lined one wall and was his pride and joy. During one of my trips to Japan, Tom made the bookcase using no nails, just precisely cut boards, and he couldn't wait to show it to me when I arrived home.

The girls were all married by then, and they and their spouses and the grandchildren soon filled the house. I slept on the couch in the living room, next to the casket, and it felt just right. Deb arrived with a pin with the motto, "Question Authority" which she attached to the inside of Tom's lapel. Tom never felt shy about questioning the experts. He was always polite about it, but his persistence sometimes made me wish I were somewhere else than sitting next to him and obviously married to him.

We had the funeral at home, too, though unlike the wake, the funeral was just for family, which more than filled the living room. My granddaughter, Michelle, sat on my lap, giving me the warm body I needed to hold. The eulogy given by the minister from our church, who knew Tom well, underscored the family man that Tom was. I invited those present to add any memories of Tom they would like to share. Aware of Tom's curiosity, my brother Charles said, "I can hear Tom repeating, 'Oh that's how this works, and this is why that happens,' excited to finally get an explanation as the wonders of the universe are revealed." Everyone who knew Tom could relate to that.

The funeral was everything we needed. As they said their goodbyes, no one was rushed away from the casket. They could stand there as long as they needed to. And after it was over, we all felt such unexpected joy, as if Tom had been liberated to go where he needed to go next. Even the funeral director, who stayed in the kitchen during the service, told me he didn't know that "a funeral could be like this," and he would never again try to talk someone out of having a wake or funeral at home.

Tom was cremated as we knew he wanted to be. We decided to spread his ashes in New England where he grew up, with the help of one of my sons-in-law and his acrobatic airplane. The spreading of the ashes is a whole story in itself, for another time.

I never thought of Tom's death as the tragedy that many people called it. I told the children that if it was time for Dad to move on, then it was also time for the rest of us to learn to live without his physical presence. God wasn't punishing us by taking their father, while rewarding their dad with heaven.

Still, learning to live without my life mate of 32 years was not easy. Even though I accepted the separation, it was years before I felt like a whole person again and not as if part of me had been torn away. Fortunately,

I still had the two boys at home. They had the same dry humor as their dad and could find laughter in the smallest things. The girls were sensitive to the smallest indication of sadness in my voice. I remember one phone call when I was pretending to be just fine. A half hour later, Allison, the daughter I had been talking to, was at the door. "Mom, you didn't sound like you were fine."

And then there were the letters and phone calls from LLL Leaders around the world. By sharing me with the world, Tom gave our family the support and prayers we needed to get through a difficult time, and we thanked him for that.

Soon Brian graduated from college and was offered a job in California. As things broke down in the house, I realized that without Tom to fix them, I couldn't afford to hire people for the job. So maybe it was time to sell the house and get an apartment.

Our house of many memories

This wasn't an easy decision to make. No one wanted to lose the home where so many important events had taken place. I kept asking God for a sign that the decision was a right one. Then one evening I drove home and before I could get out of the car, I watched the gutters peel off the entire house. I took that as God's confirmation!

I would have liked to move back into the city near Lincoln Park where I grew up, but the area had changed from a middle class neighborhood to a much more upscale one. So my daughter Deb suggested I visit a friend of hers who lived in Evanston. I did. She gave me a local newspaper to check out places to live, and I've been happily living in Evanston now for more than 20 years.

First Christmas in Evanston

It was another right decision because my children and grandchildren love coming to Evanston. You can get to Chicago by el, train, or bus, all of them just blocks from where I live, so my apartment has become a great stopover place for family coming and going to the city. When I had to find work, I got a job managing Rosie, a unique and classy toy store in town, after stopping there to buy a present for a grandchild. I also have made wonderful friends through my meditation group and book club. Northwestern University, parks, and Lake Michigan are just down the street. It's a great place to live!

For the first time in my life, I have been living alone. I've never been against marrying again, but my life has been so busy that until recently I didn't have much time to think about it. With the right man, it would be nice. But Tom did set the bar pretty high!

A New Beginning

Tom died in early November. When Thanksgiving arrived later that month, I was on my own for the very first time preparing Thanksgiving dinner for the family. It was a surprise to discover that getting the turkey ready, cooking the giblets for gravy, and preparing the dressing was so much easier than when Tom and I did it together!

You might have to be married to an engineer like Tom to understand, but with engineers, projects are thought out carefully and precisely. Everything has to be done in order and on time. While such an approach is more likely to guarantee a good result, it can put a lot of pressure on people who are less meticulous when it comes to cooking, like me.

But there was much around the house that only Tom could do. Hardly a day passed without me wanting to check with him about something. I was so lucky having the two boys still living at home to do some of those "manly" jobs.

And while I wasn't feeling sorry for myself, there would be the unexpected tearing up when a favorite song of Tom's would come on the radio. There was the clench of my stomach each month as I sat down to pay the bills, hoping with my reduced income, that I had enough to cover them. It's not my nature to moan over what might have been, but that first year I couldn't help but look back as we celebrated certain milestones, remembering that Tom had been there the previous year. But all in all, I felt I was handling things pretty well. It was my children who could see how distracted I was and how difficult I found it to focus on anything.

But life moves on. 1981 had already brought another big change into my life. Earlier that year, the LLLI Board of Directors voted to eliminate the position of president, so I no longer had that responsibility. I was offered the job of Editor of a new magazine, *American Mother*. That looked promising, but changed when the publisher died a few months later before the magazine had a chance to get off the ground.

Then a group of doctors attending births outside the hospital asked me to be the Executive Director of the newly formed Alternative Birth Crisis Coalition. ABCC provided legal counsel and expert assistance to prosecuted alternative birth practitioners, and membership in ABCC helped support that work. The Coalition helped physicians and midwives during the next four years.

Since 1977, I had also been writing a column, "Another View," that appeared on the back page in Dr. Robert Mendelsohn's monthly newsletter, *The People's Doctor*. This job would continue until Dr. Mendelsohn's death in 1988. Doing the research necessary to write that column was an education in itself. Each issue focused on a particular health challenge, and while Dr. Mendelsohn covered the research and medical perspective, I wrote from the perspective of a mother and layperson. It was a dream job because I was given total freedom to say what I wanted, even if I disagreed with the doctor.

I especially liked writing columns where I compared the treatments used in different approaches for the same disease. Why did all these different treatments work? What might they have in common? It's a question I still ask myself today when checking out the many nutritional approaches to good health. Some of them totally contradict each other: starches vs. no starches, fish oil vs. no oil, meat vs. no meat. Yet, with each plan, doctors can point to people whose lives were saved and whose diseases disappeared when their particular program was followed.

In 1990, I was invited to appear on NBC television's *Night of 100 Stars III,* as part of a segment honoring a group of individuals and organizations who had made significant contributions to the world. As a benefit for The Actor's Fund, the show was being taped at Radio City Music Hall in New York City and was to be seen around the world. Other honorees were Dr. Benjamin Spock, an American pediatrician whose book *Baby and Child Care* is one of the biggest sellers of all time; Clara Hale, founder of Hale House in Harlem, which takes care of cocaine babies; Elie Wiesel, Holocaust survivor and author; Ralph Nader, consumer advocate; Buzz Aldrin, astronaut; and Mathilde Krim, AIDS researcher.

The honorees and a companion were sent first class plane tickets. I chose Hugh Riordan, MD, a member of LLLI's Professional Advisory Board and husband of LLL Leader Jan Riordan, RN, as my companion. Hugh, who lived in Wichita, Kansas, had volunteered to head LLLI's Capital Campaign to raise money to purchase a much needed larger headquarters, and we hoped that by attending the event he might meet some potential donors.

I had been sent a script ahead of time and saw that in the Award segment, Walter Cronkite would be introducing me. That was exciting! The next day I wandered into Radio City Music Hall for the dress rehearsal. I didn't realize when I sat down that I was right across the aisle from the director of the show, so when Walter Cronkite and Leslie Stahl came in to pick up their scripts, they stood right next to me. That's why, as Walter Cronkite read his script, I was able to hear him say, "Breastfeeding! I can't say breastfeeding." Leslie Stahl, as his co-introducer, jumped right in to rescue him and assured Mr. Cronkite that she would introduce me, and he wouldn't have to say that word.

But when we did a run through of the award segment on stage, Ms. Stahl seemed to have trouble reading the monitor for my introduction, and she promised she would memorize it before the show was taped that evening.

The large dressing room I was assigned to was shared with stars I had only seen on the movie or television screens before. They included Gladys Knight, Loretta Lynne and her sister, Crystal Gayle, and Carol Channing. Katherine Hepburn and Jane Fonda were in the dressing room next door. Betty White struck me as one of the friendliest people, as she sat and patiently listened to anyone who came up to talk to her.

Backstage with Gladys Knight

Back stage, I walked past Sylvester Stallone, Michael Caine, Mel Torme, and shared a bench with Jimmy Stewart, while eavesdropping on Mohammed Ali who sat across from us. Ed Asner gave me a hug. Dick Cavett was my partner for our appearance before the media. Elie Weisel told me that he felt LLLI had made a much more significant contribution to the world than he had ever done. At the gala dinner, I told Dr. Spock, who was celebrating his 87th birthday, that he had sent me a letter years ago with cash in it to cover the cost of the very first edition of the *Womanly Art*. "You are lucky I sent you money," he laughed. "We doctors expect to get things for free."

A hug from Ed Asner

Talking with Dr. and Mrs. Spock

And then around midnight, it was time to tape the Awards segment before a packed theater audience. But again my introduction was fumbled. They tried to fix it later with a voiceover, but it didn't work, so the entire segment, with the honorees and their companions flown in from around the country, was deleted from the show. All because Walter Cronkite–once dubbed "the most trusted man in America," the man who broke the news to the world that President John F. Kennedy had been assassinated–was too embarrassed to say "breastfeeding."

Taking Another Look at HIV and Breastfeeding

In 1997, I once again found myself going down a road I hardly knew existed, let alone one that I could have imagined traveling on. That year, the World Health Organization issued a draft proposal, "HIV and Infant Feeding: A Review of HIV Transmission through Breastfeeding." While acknowledging the role of breastmilk in protecting infants against disease, it stated that "The most effective method of preventing breastmilk transmission of HIV is breastmilk avoidance." This countered WHO's previous recommendation that the decision as to whether or not an HIV-positive mother should breastfeed her baby was to be made on a case by case basis. This new proposal prodded LLL Leader Mary Lofton and me to find the scientific research validating this recommendation.

I thought it would be a simple matter. All we had to do was ask scientists for the new studies proving that babies breastfed by HIV-positive mothers were more likely to get sick and die than babies who were fed formula. But it turned out not to be that simple. I got vague replies to my queries: "Some study in Africa," or laundry lists of references from published research papers, none of which answered the question. And we learned there was disagreement among mainstream scientists as to what these studies actually proved.

Although breastfeeding by an HIV-positive mother in the United States was not against the law, she might have her baby put in foster care if the authorities found out about it. There were even concerns that an LLL Leader might be accused of breaking the law if she helped an HIV-positive mother to breastfeed.

Some researchers pointed out there was no proof of infectious HIV virus in breastmilk. Nor had HIV virus ever been isolated in human milk. While the agencies they worked for promoted the mainstream view, some of these scientists had too much to lose by going public with their doubts, and they encouraged our examination of the issue.

We discovered there were at least three belief systems in play here. There was the mainstream belief that HIV caused AIDS and breastfeeding increased a baby's chance of getting AIDS. A subset of this belief came from those who pointed out that while HIV caused AIDS, there was no proof of live HIV virus in breastmilk, or if there was, there was uncertainty about whether there was enough to infect the baby. And then there were the two other belief systems among researchers—one group believed that HIV, a retrovirus, could not cause AIDS, and another group who found no proof of the presence of HIV! The more we looked into it, the more we realized the assumptions about breastfeeding and HIV/AIDS needed to be more carefully examined and validated.

It just so happened that the following year I was asked to go to South Africa as the leader of a People to People Breastfeeding Delegation. It provided an unexpected opportunity to meet with health professionals and activists deeply concerned about this issue. The very first day we made a trip to Baragawanth, the largest hospital in the world, in the Soweto area of Johannesburg. As we walked into the Pediatric section of the hospital, we saw a mural on the wall depicting a mother saddened by her baby's illness, presumably AIDS, and then in the next panel, with a smile on her face giving the baby a very large bottle of milk. We were proudly told by the doctor in charge that every baby in that hospital, breastfed or not, got a bottle with something in it. Later, she gave a talk, complete with slides, giving formula-feeding as the answer to preventing AIDS in babies. When I asked a few simple questions, she got upset and responded by asking, "Mrs. Tompson, if you had AIDS, would you breastfeed your baby?" I had to honestly answer that if she had asked me that question a few years ago, my answer would have been of course not, but today, having found no proof existed that breastfeeding was harmful, I would breastfeed my baby.

Health workers who were also accredited as LLL peer counselors, singing
the songs they used to teach mothers about breastfeeding

Apparently, the word of my reply, which made some LLL people nervous, got out, and when we reached Cape Town and toured yet another hospital, the matron in charge asked if I would give a talk about breastfeeding and HIV. At the end of the tour, we stepped into a large room where an audience was already waiting, and I had a chance to share with them the things I had learned.

At the time, much of the data on the spread of the disease were extrapolated from the periodic testing of pregnant women in Africa using the Elisa test. However, there was no allowance for, nor often awareness of, the fact that not only could pregnancy itself cause a false positive, but that in central Africa, microbes responsible for tuberculosis, malaria, and leprosy were so prevalent that because of the non-specificity of the test, the general population registered over 70 percent false positive results.

In the clinics servicing the shanty towns we visited, there was no money for testing for HIV antibodies or for treatment. When I got back home, I suggested to an international agency that this would be the perfect opportunity to keep records on the health of the mother and their babies born at the clinic as a kind of natural history. Assuming that a certain percentage of the mothers were HIV-positive, they could track their health and healthcare without introducing confounding factors, like the non-specificity of the test, the effect on a person's immune system when they are told they have a fatal and socially embarrassing disease, and the unanswerable question when someone died as to whether they were killed by the very toxic medicines or the disease.

I was told that if there was money to keep such records, it would be unethical not to use the money for testing and medication.

I found myself needing money, too. I was working at several part-time jobs at the time, so it would be easier to take time off for family gatherings. I was finding it necessary to spend more time at home to stay in touch with the people involved in breastfeeding and AIDS. Talking on the phone with scientists and researchers was only possible during the day, and I had to be there when they were available to talk.

With the help of Peggy O'Mara and *Mothering* magazine, we set up a luncheon in Santa Fe during a LLLI Physician's Seminar and invited doctors from the first two belief systems. I also took advantage of being in Santa Fe to visit with Alice Ladas. It was Alice's graduate school thesis, many years earlier, on the "Relationship of Information and Support to Outcome of Breastfeeding" that first documented the effectiveness of LLLI's work. I told Alice about my work gathering information on breastfeeding and AIDS, and she immediately offered to give me a substantial check, the first financial gift from friends and supporters that would keep this cause going through the years.

I was concerned that there wasn't any kind of control group of babies being breastfed by HIV-positive mothers used to compare outcomes from babies formula-fed by HIV-positive mothers. So I established a small registry of HIV-positive breastfeeding moms who were brave enough to let me know they had breastfed and who periodically filled out a questionnaire about their health and that of their babies. When I told someone from the National Institute of Health about these natural histories, concern was expressed that I might be put in jail if it was thought I had encouraged these mothers to breastfeed. That's how confused the situation was. I had been contacted by the mothers after they made the decision, so I didn't let that possibility stop me from gathering such important information.

During those first two years, I met with researchers at Georgetown University Medical, the National Institutes of Health, the FDA, congressional aides, and directors of government agencies. I met and talked with former president Jimmy Carter, telling him how I wished I had his skills in conflict resolution to bring together the different belief systems found in the AIDS community. President Carter admitted that it was a difficult situation and gave me a copy of his book, *The Turning Point*, which is rooted in his vision of how people of good faith can right the wrongs of our society.

But the dialogue needed to be enlarged, and in 2000, with long-time LLL Leader Karen Zeretzke's expert help and her suggestion of a very appropriate name, AnotherLook, a private chat list was set up. I sent out 45 invitations to researchers, health professionals, an HIV-positive mother, speakers, and others interested in the issue, and within minutes I had responses from people belonging to differing belief systems. In less than two weeks, we had subscribers in South Africa, Zimbabwe, Sweden, Canada, Great Britain, and the United States.

As one subscriber later wrote, "I am very pleased that AnotherLook exists. It is one of the few places where the 'great divide,' in terms of views on HIV/AIDS is crossed. I am pleased that civilized discussions continue between people despite these views, and that we can cooperate where we agree and not get all bent out of shape when we disagree."

Despite my foot dragging with establishing another not-for-profit, I finally had to admit that doing so would give AnotherLook more credibility and enable us to raise much needed tax deductible funds, so in 2001, AnotherLook became a not-for-profit. When Alice Ladas gave us that first gift, I thought that by giving up my part-time jobs and working from home, we would get the information needed in two months. But instead we've kept working at gathering information, raising critical questions, and stimulating needed research about breastfeeding in the context of HIV and AIDS for the next ten years.

During that time we have had critiques of studies published in a variety of medical journals. These can be found on our website, www.anotherlook.org, along with the power points from panels presented at LLLI International Conferences. We presented a poster session at the International AIDS Conference in Toronto, round table sessions at an American Public Health Association Annual meeting, presentations at Breastfeeding Coalition Conferences hosted by the United States Breastfeeding Committee, and have been invited to present talks at LLL-hosted Health Provider Seminars in many different countries.

In the AnotherLook Call to Action, we point out that current research, policy, and practice are often based on fear and are focused on the reduction of HIV transmission, while neglecting the impact on morbidity and mortality. This not only may be misleading, but may inadvertently set back critical gains already achieved in public health as a result of the protection and promotion of breastfeeding.

That these concerns were taken to heart by others became apparent in 2010, when WHO came out with a new recommendation that all HIV-positive mothers, with appropriate medication, should exclusively breastfeed their babies for six months, with breastfeeding continuing after that along with the supplementation of other foods.

In ten years, we have come full circle. AnotherLook has had its impact, and attitudes are changing. We set out to get people talking and to find some answers, and the organization has done its job. WHO's new recommendations take into account morbidity and mortality and are no longer based exclusively on virus transmission. We never were able to find the funding for research that would tell us if HIV virus in breastmilk is actually infectious. The chat list and the website will continue. But AnotherLook will no longer be a not-for-profit after 2011.

Breastfeeding and HIV presented a challenge to me that I couldn't ignore. As author, composer, and astrologer Dane Rudhyar once said, "When you don't follow your nature, there is a hole in the universe where you are supposed to be." I found myself compelled to fill that hole.

Circle of Life

They say time flies and I believe it now.

It seems like the blink of an eye since Tom and I met, got married, and started having babies. "Turn Around," is a song that expresses this so poignantly with "Turn around and you're two, turn around and you're four, turn around and you're a young girl going out of the door."

Our children grew up, most graduated from college, all but one have married, and when Deb became the first to get pregnant, she and her husband made the decision to come back to our house to have the baby. What a wonderful tradition that became!

The only time birth at mom and dad's became a bit challenging to navigate was when Deb was expecting her second baby around the same time Allison and Mike were planning to get married. Both events were to take place at our home.

What were the chances of them happening on the same day? Miniscule, I thought, and put it out of my head. But on the morning of the wedding, while we were still in bed, Deb called to tell us she was in labor. She asked us not to tell anyone because she didn't want to upstage her sister's wedding.

So after an hour and a half drive, Deb arrived at our house, all dressed up, wearing high heels and amazingly able to mask any hints of having contractions. The wedding went off in the backyard as planned. Food was served at round tables under a large tent.

Allison and Mike Fagerholm with Tom and me

As the wedding guests and bride and groom departed, Deb retired to our bed, freshly changed from when Tom and I got up that morning, Dr. White was called, and before the evening was over, Kelly was born. As Allison and Mike left that night, we told them about the impending birth, so the next morning, before leaving on their honeymoon camping trip, they came back to greet their brand new niece.

Kelly Dotson, now a mother herself, Jordan, baby Christian, and Justin

I can't think of a better way to become a grandmother than being present at your grandchild's birth. I've met women and men who found being seen as a grandparent threatening to their image, whatever that image was. It has been my experience that being there to greet and hold that baby glues you to that child forever. During the next few days in any encounter I had, even with strangers asking for directions, I had to tell them about my grandchild's birth.

But after Tom's death, grandchildren were born who had never met their grandfather. So one day, probably with her father whispering in her ear, our daughter Allison suggested we have a celebration of Tom's life and spend a day, "Remembering Dad."

It gave us a chance to introduce Tom to the younger grandchildren and share our "Dad" stories. We got together at Allison and Mike's home one afternoon. I made a collage of photos of Tom that started when he was in grammar school. It was interesting to see the resemblance in his childhood pictures to some of our grandsons. We played music Tom liked and showed slides of our camping trips and other family activities. Everyone was welcome to stand up and share a favorite memory. I like to think that Tom was listening and enjoyed the day, too.

In 1990, my mother died at the age of 84. She had been a widow since my dad's death in his sleep, 26 years earlier. My mother was an amazingly healthy person. Earlier that year, she began suffering from what was diagnosed as a pinched nerve. Nothing seemed to help alleviate her pain, so she insisted on having an MRI, which clearly showed lung cancer that had spread to her brain. My mother had never smoked in her life, but both her father and her husband did. Interestingly, neither her dad nor my dad was ever diagnosed with lung cancer. Outside of the cancer, she was in such good health that the doctors decided she should come to the hospital as an outpatient for radiation and get chemotherapy through a port. The objective was to shrink the tumor in her brain and make her more comfortable, which was all they could do.

I was managing the toy store in Evanston then and because the owner was out of the country, I had to be there every day to keep the store open. So I moved into my mom's house to be with her at night, and then go with her to the hospital for her outpatient treatments in the morning before making the drive to Evanston. Allen Jackson, who had been unofficially adopted by my parents when he came out of the orphanage, and his wife, Mary, offered to help by doing the driving. A home helper was secured to be with my mother during the day until I got back from work.

Family came by to visit and bring treats that might tempt Mom's appetite, but I could see that she was losing ground. On the day the toy store owners returned, I called home and learned that she had gone to bed. My mother hardly ever went to bed during the day. I knew something was really wrong, and I knew I had to get back to my mother.

So I left work and got to her house to find her lying in bed, almost comatose. I called the doctor to tell him I thought she was in the process of dying in case there was anything I should do to make her more comfortable. He said he would be over later.

So I sat beside the bed. Her arm closest to me was cold and had been for days. But when I put my hands on her arm to warm it, she sort of shrugged, and I suddenly realized from my experience of sitting with women in labor that she was in the process of dying, and I was distracting her by touching her. But I wanted her to know I was there with her, so I started singing. And what came out of my mouth were lullabies! Mother was lying in a semi-reclining position when she suddenly began to sit up. I got on the bed beside her as she came into my arms. And she died.

Even now, writing this 21 years later, with tears in my eyes, I feel so blessed, so lucky to have been with my mother when she died in my arms at home.

My mom and dad

———

Time. It's a funny thing. When Melanie, our first baby was born, and Tom and I were trying to get the hang of being parents, we were told that it would take about three months to figure it out. Three months! That seemed like such a long time that they might as well have said three years.

But except for those first three months with our first baby, life has pretty much flown by. And with the passage of time, it has become abundantly clear to me that making the world a better place by our presence, unconditionally loving those who share our lives, and cherishing those who cross our path, is all that really matters after all.

Epilogue: Lucky Me!

"Marian. I've heard you are semi-retired, but I really don't believe it," my friend, Greg, wrote a few days ago. "Semi-retired?" I wanted to respond, "I never was aware I was semi-retired. Guess I've just been too busy to notice."

I do work each day in my office at home. There is AnotherLook to take care of, upcoming conferences where I'll be speaking, research to catch up on, phone calls to return, and all those emails. As diligent as I am about answering emails, it is difficult to get below the usual 2500 that always seem to be sitting in my inbox. In fact, there are never enough hours in my day to handle everything needing to be done.

Maybe the perception that I'm semi-retired came from my resignation as an LLL Leader in 2010. It was a decision that was not easy to make, but I felt that my dissatisfaction with the way LLLI was being managed left me no choice. The space left by that change was soon filled with other work.

There are also fun things I look forward to, like the twice-weekly yoga classes at the senior center, and when the weather is nice, walking in the park and along the lake.

Every month, there is the book club I've been part of for more than 20 years. Our meditation group that used to meet twice a month is now only able to get together once a month, and it's not for meditation, but for conversation over a delicious potluck lunch. I see my LLL friends who live in the area at our monthly movie and meal at a restaurant. We are so eager to see each other that anyone who is short of time and can't make the movie will still join the group for dinner.

My children and grown grandchildren come by to give a hand when needed or just to visit and enjoy each other's company. My grandson Matt spent time living with me after graduating from college, so he could take the nearby El train downtown for meetings and interviews. I loved the evenings when we would be sitting facing each other, on opposite sides of my desk, both busy at our computers. As a movie reviewer, conversations with Matt taught me a lot about film. On Christmas, we still have brunch at my apartment for the children and their spouses, grandchildren, great grandchildren, and my brother, and the delight at being together far outweighs the crowded rooms.

It's a good life.

I believe that we are all connected and that we are each an expression of God. (With that in mind, standing in those long lines at the airport, waiting to go through security can be a fascinating experience.) Our choices impact people we might never meet. I believe we have more control over our lives than we sometimes realize because our thoughts do affect our reality and we can choose our thoughts.

I believe I'm one of the luckiest people in the world, with family and friends from all over the globe who have enriched my life in so many different ways. Though they weren't spoiled as children, my grown children spoil me all the time.

It isn't always easy being one of the "first" to take a particular path. Knowing what it means to have the support of even one friend makes this quote by G.K. Chesterton, one of my favorites:

> There are no words to express the abyss between isolation and having one ally. It may be conceded to the mathematicians that four is twice two. But two is not twice one; two is two thousand times one.

When it came to writing this book, which was a "first" for me, I was doubly blessed. Melissa, this book would *never* have happened without you, your expertise, your diligence, your status charts, and your sense of humor. Thank you for agreeing to be part of a journey that took much longer than either of us expected. Kaye, you were our gift beyond measure, as you read through multiple drafts, catching typos, and making valuable suggestions as to content.

It truly has been a passionate journey *and* an unexpected life. Can't wait to see what comes next!

Marian's Personal Legacy

"What is it like to have Marian Tompson as your mother?" The children have been asked this question countless times over the years. Those "children," now in their 40's, 50's, and 60's, are delighted to share their mother with you from a perspective that only they have.

Melanie Tompson Kandler:

It really struck me at the banquet for La Leche League's 50th anniversary that Mom was only 26 years old when she sat under that tree with Mary White at the picnic in Elmhurst, Illinois. Twenty-six. At that age I had just been married. Eight years after that picnic, I witnessed Betty Friedan scolding my mother for her backwards ideas that were keeping women in their homes taking care of their families instead of experiencing the world. Looking at the empowerment that La Leche League has given women around the world by understanding the value of our intuition and experience when we raise our families, I can be proud of her part in a real modern women's movement.

Deborah Tompson Frueh:

Mom never ever discouraged our reactions to life. The biggest compliment that I can give to my mother is that she somehow allowed each of us to be who we are. She didn't try to mold us or push us, but she always seemed to know about the things we were interested in and encouraged each of us in our various interests. To me, that's no small feat. Living that and then having children of my own, I can only hope that I was able to do the same for my children because looking back, that was the gift I cherished most of all from Mom.

Allison Tompson Fagerholm:

It has always been my goal to "be like my mom when I grow up"! My goal continues to this day despite my mom's grand age of 81 and mine of 59! Mom has friends and associates all over the world—which she continues to travel across even to this day. Mom's energy amazes me, as well as her many varied interests and her depth of knowledge in each.

I am continually grateful that my mom opened our minds and our lives to alternative choices. I feel confident in speaking for my siblings when I say that none of us are afraid to "think outside the box" when life throws us a curve ball! Coupling that philosophy along with our dad's motto to question authority…the options are limitless!

If I could boil everything down into one feeling, I would have to say that my mom's greatest legacy in my life is learning to never be afraid to "swim up-stream"—never be afraid to handle things in life differently than the majority does. Being somewhat of a renegade has always appealed to me because of growing up in a household that advocated breastfeeding in a world that placed a higher value on manufactured, convenience products. What could be more convenient than breastfeeding, or more natural, and certainly more nourishing?

Laurel Tompson Davies:

Mom has NOT ceased to amaze me with her endeavor to continually help other women around the world. If you'd ask me what I'd like to be when I grow up? Well, like my mom! Having seen my mom speak before people, I found myself feeling comfortable in front of people, too. I have a strong desire to travel the world like my mom. Most importantly, my hopes are that I have created memories for MY son to look back on. . . .

Sheila Tompson Doucet:

My mother was invited to speak about raising children to the Home Economics class for the seniors at my high school. I was an underclassman, but got permission to go to the class and listen to my mom. I pretty much felt that this was all going to be what I'd heard before, but once again, Mom blew me away.

One of the girls asked my mother how you discipline children. Well, without missing a beat, my mother answered, "If you look at the root word of discipline, it's 'disciple.' And a disciple is a person who follows someone. So in order to discipline a child, you need to act in a way that you would like them to follow."

Just like that, my mother defined who she is as a person, what her beliefs are, how she respects everyone, including children, how we all have the right to choose, and the right to be led if we so choose.

Brian Tompson:

Being the first son after five daughters, I held a special place in the Tompson family. I learned engineering, home repair, and respect for tools at my Dad's knee. I also learned skepticism; show me, explain it, and tell me why. Mom, on the other hand, taught me openness, acceptance of the unknown, and spirituality. I consider myself an open-minded skeptic—a very useful mindset as I travel though life.

The worlds I lived in all were a result of Mom and what she did, and how she raised us. I really don't have "Mom defining" memories. Instead she was omnipresent, enabling and allowing each of us to become the people we became. Back in the day of single income families, Mom was at home with us every day. As La Leche League grew, and travel became part of Mom's routine, the great and close family she created, allowed me to wave happily at her departures, and more happily at her returns.

Philip Tompson:

In the end I have to say that Mom is probably the closest I will ever see to someone who is truly altruistic. With a heart and mindset firmly based in helping others and enjoying life, Mom taught me without even trying that going a little out of your way to help others can make a huge difference to thousands of people or just one. In the end, it doesn't matter how many, as long as your heart and your intent were pure.

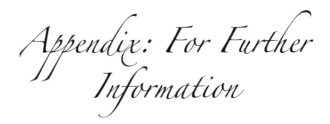

Appendix: For Further Information

AnotherLook

www.anotherlook.org

La Leche League International

www.llli.org

To read more about the history of La Leche League:

DePaul University, Chicago, IL

La Leche League Papers, Special Collections, and Archives Department
http://library.depaul.edu/Collections/collectionsList.aspx?s=98
archives@depaul.edu
773-325-2167

La Leche League at the Crossroads of Medicine, Feminism, and Religion, by Jule DeJager Ward. (University of North Carolina Press, 2000)

LLLove Story, by Kaye Lowman (La Leche League International, 1977; out of print)

The Revolutionaries Wore Pearls, by Kaye Lowman (La Leche League International, 2007)

Seven Voices, One Dream, by Mary Ann Cahill (La Leche League International, 2001)

Author Bios

Marian Leonard Tompson is best known as one of the Founders of La Leche League International, serving as its President for 24 years. Wife of the late Clement (Tom) Tompson, she is the mother of seven, grandmother of seventeen and great grandmother of nine.

Julie Kaplan

Marian's writing career began with her column, "Did You Know," which appeared in her high school newspaper. Since then, she has co-authored the first two editions of the best-selling Womanly Art of Breastfeeding and was the first editor of two LLLI publications, *New Beginnings* (originally *LLL News*) and *Leaven*. She has written forwards for numerous books and has had articles published in a variety of professional journals including *Padiatrie and Padologie* (Austria), *Environmental Child Health*, *The American Journal of Clinical Nutrition* and *The West Indian Medical Journal*. From 1977-1988 she wrote a monthly column for Dr. Robert Mendelsohn's newsletter, *The People's Doctor*.

Through the years Marian has been a member of numerous advisory committees and organizations including the United States Breastfeeding Committee, The World Alliance of Breastfeeding Action, the Alternative Birth Crisis Coalition, and the National Association of Parents and Professionals for Safe Alternatives in Childbirth, all of which reflect her commitment to providing information and support for breastfeeding mothers and their babies. In 2001 she founded AnotherLook, a not for profit organization dedicated to gathering information, raising critical questions and stimulating needed research about HIV and AIDS as they relate to breastfeeding.

Melissa Clark Vickers, mother of two grown children, is a writer, International Board Certified Lactation Consultant, and long-time La Leche League Leader. She taught high school biology until the birth of her son Dan in 1983. When her second child, Merrilee, was a year old and not sleeping through the night, in desperation Melissa attended her first LLL meeting in Marietta, Georgia, where she found not only support  for breastfeeding, but also for a parenting style that resonated with her instincts that said to ignore "conventional wisdom" and instead focus on meeting the needs of her child. She became a LLL Leader in 1990, and resumed her "teaching" career—only this time by helping other mothers discover the satisfaction that comes from parenting from the heart.

Melissa also discovered a love of writing through LLL, and has written for various international, national, regional, and local publications in and out of LLL. She currently edits the United States Lactation Consultant Association's monthly *eNews*, and writes for baby gooroo (www.babygooroo.com). In addition, she works extensively with Family Voices, a national grassroots advocacy organization for families of children with special health care needs (www.familyvoices.org). She participated on the American Academy of Pediatrics Infancy Panel for the 2008 revision of Bright Futures: Guidelines for Health Supervision of Infants, Children, and Adolescents, 3rd Edition.

Melissa and her husband, Bob, live in rural west Tennessee.

Ordering Information

Hale Publishing, L.P.

1712 N. Forest Street

Amarillo, Texas, USA 79106

8:00 am to 5:00 pm CST

Call » 806.376.9900

Toll free » 800.378.1317

Fax » 806.376.9901

Online Orders

www.ibreastfeeding.com